THIRD EDITION

TOP NOTCH 2A

ENGLISH FOR TODAY'S WORLD

with Workbook

JOAN SASLOW
ALLEN ASCHER

With *Top Notch Pop* Songs and Karaoke
by Rob Morsberger

Top Notch: English for Today's World   Level 2A with Workbook, Third Edition

Pearson Education, 10 Bank Street, White Plains, NY 10606 USA

Staff credits: The people who made up the *Top Notch* team are Pietro Alongi, Rhea Banker, Peter Benson, Tracey Munz Cataldo, Rosa Chapinal, Aerin Csigay, Dave Dickey, Gina DiLillo, Nancy Flaggman, Irene Frankel, Shelley Gazes, Christopher Leonowicz, Kate McLoughlin, Julie Molnar, Laurie Neaman, Sherri Pemberton, Pamela Pia, Jennifer Raspiller, Charlene Straub, Paula Van Ells, and Kenneth Volcjak.

Cover photo: Sprint/Corbis
Text composition: TSI Graphics

Library of Congress Cataloging-in-Publication Data

Saslow, Joan M.
  Top Notch : English for today's world. Fundamentals / Joan Saslow, Allen Ascher ; With Top Notch Pop Songs
  and Karaoke by Rob Morsberger. — Third Edition.
      pages cm
  Includes biographical references.
  ISBN 978-0-13-354275-2 — ISBN 978-0-13-339348-4 — ISBN 978-0-13-354277-6 — ISBN 978-0-13-354278-3   1. English language—
  Textbooks for foreign speakers. 2. English language—Problems, exercises, etc. 3. English language—Sound recordings for foreign speakers.
  I. Ascher, Allen. II. Morsberger, Robert Eustis, 1929- III. Title. IV. Title: English for today's world.
  PE1128.S2757 2015
  428.2'4--dc23

                    2013044020

Printed in the United States of America
ISBN-10: 0-13-381927-2
ISBN-13: 978-0-13-381927-4
7 17

pearsonelt.com/topnotch3e

In Memoriam

Rob Morsberger (1959–2013)

The authors wish to acknowledge their memory of and gratitude to **Rob Morsberger**, the gifted composer and songwriter of the *Top Notch Pop* Songs and Karaoke that have provided learners both language practice and pleasure.

Contents

LEARNING OBJECTIVES

	COMMUNICATION GOALS	VOCABULARY	GRAMMAR

UNIT 1
Getting Acquainted
PAGE 2
	• Get reacquainted with someone
	• Greet a visitor to your country
	• Discuss gestures and customs
	• Describe an interesting experience
		• Tourist activities
		• The hand
		• Participial adjectives
			• The present perfect
			  ◦ Statements and yes / no questions
			  ◦ Form and usage
			  ◦ Past participles of irregular verbs
			  ◦ With already, yet, ever, before, and never
			
			GRAMMAR BOOSTER
			• The present perfect
			  ◦ Information questions
			  ◦ Yet and already: expansion, common errors
			  ◦ Ever, never, and before: use and placement

UNIT 2
Going to the Movies
PAGE 14
	• Apologize for being late
	• Discuss preferences for movie genres
	• Describe and recommend movies
	• Discuss effects of movie violence on viewers
		• Explanations for being late
		• Movie genres
		• Adjectives to describe movies
			• The present perfect
			  ◦ With for and since
			  ◦ Other uses
			• Wants and preferences: would like and would rather
			  ◦ Form and usage
			  ◦ Statements, questions, and answers
			
			GRAMMAR BOOSTER
			• The present perfect continuous
			• The present participle: spelling
			• Expressing preferences: review, expansion, and common errors

UNIT 3
Staying in Hotels
PAGE 26
	• Leave and take a message
	• Check into a hotel
	• Request housekeeping services
	• Choose a hotel
		• Hotel room types and kinds of beds
		• Hotel room amenities and services
			• The future with will
			  ◦ Form and usage
			  ◦ Statements and questions
			  ◦ Contractions
			• The real conditional
			  ◦ Form and usage
			  ◦ Statements and questions
			
			GRAMMAR BOOSTER
			• Will: expansion
			• Can, should, and have to: future meaning
			• The real conditinal: factual and future; usage and common errors

UNIT 4
Cars and Driving
PAGE 38
	• Discuss a car accident
	• Describe a car problem
	• Rent a car
	• Discuss good and bad driving
		• Bad driving habits
		• Car parts
		• Ways to respond (with concern / relief)
		• Phrasal verbs for talking about cars
		• Car types
		• Driving behavior
			• The past continuous
			  ◦ Form and usage
			  ◦ Vs. the simple past tense
			• Direct objects with phrasal verbs
			
			GRAMMAR BOOSTER
			• The past continuous: other uses
			• Nouns and pronouns: review

UNIT 5
Personal Care and Appearance
PAGE 50
	• Ask for something in a store
	• Make an appointment at a salon or spa
	• Discuss ways to improve appearance
	• Define the meaning of beauty
		• Salon services
		• Personal care products
		• Discussing beauty
			• Indefinite quantities and amounts
			  ◦ Some and any
			  ◦ A lot of / lots of, many, and much
			• Indefinite pronouns: someone / no one / anyone
			
			GRAMMAR BOOSTER
			• Some and any: indefiniteness
			• Too many, too much, and enough
			• Comparative quantifiers fewer and less
			• Indefinite pronouns: something, anything, and nothing

CONVERSATION STRATEGIES	LISTENING / PRONUNCIATION	READING	WRITING
• Use "I don't think so." to soften a negative answer • Say "I know!" to exclaim that you've discovered an answer • Use "Welcome to ___." to greet someone in a new place • Say "That's great." to acknowledge someone's positive experience	**Listening Skills** • Listen to classify • Listen for details **Pronunciation** • Sound reduction in the present perfect	**Texts** • A poster about world customs • A magazine article about non-verbal communication • A travel poster • A photo story **Skills/strategies** • Identify supporting details • Relate to personal experience	**Task** • Write a description of an interesting experience **WRITING BOOSTER** • Avoiding run-on sentences
• Apologize and provide a reason when late • Say "That's fine." to reassure • Offer to repay someone with "How much do I owe?" • Use "What would you rather do . . . ?" to ask about preference • Soften a negative response with "To tell you the truth, . . ."	**Listening Skills** • Listen for main ideas • Listen to infer • Dictation **Pronunciation** • Reduction of h	**Texts** • A movie website • Movie reviews • A textbook excerpt about violence in movies • A photo story **Skills/strategies** • Understand from context • Confirm content • Evaluate ideas	**Task** • Write an essay about violence in movies and on TV **WRITING BOOSTER** • Paragraphs • Topic sentences
• Say "Would you like to leave a message?" if someone isn't available • Say "Let's see." to indicate you're checking information • Make a formal, polite request with "May I ___?" • Say "Here you go." when handing someone something • Use "By the way, . . ." to introduce new information	**Listening Skills** • Listen to take phone messages • Listen for main ideas • Listen for details **Pronunciation** • Contractions with <u>will</u>	**Texts** • Phone message slips • A hotel website • A city map • A photo story **Skills/strategies** • Draw conclusions • Identify supporting details • Interpret a map	**Task** • Write a paragraph explaining the reasons for choosing a hotel **WRITING BOOSTER** • Avoiding sentence fragments with <u>because</u> or <u>since</u>
• Express concern about another's condition after an accident • Express relief when hearing all is OK • Use "only" to minimize the seriousness of a situation • Use "actually" to soften negative information • Empathize with "I'm sorry to hear that."	**Listening Skills** • Listen for details • Listen to summarize **Pronunciation** • Stress of particles in phrasal verbs	**Texts** • A questionnaire about bad driving habits • Rental car customer profiles • A feature article about defensive driving • A driving behavior survey • A photo story **Skills/strategies** • Understand from context • Critical thinking	**Task** • Write a paragraph comparing good and bad drivers **WRITING BOOSTER** • Connecting words and sentences: <u>and</u>, <u>in addition</u>, <u>furthermore</u>, and <u>therefore</u>
• Use "Excuse me." to initiate a conversation with a salesperson • Confirm information by repeating it with rising intonation • Use "No problem." to show you don't mind an inconvenience • Use "Let me check" to ask someone to wait while you confirm information	**Listening Skills** • Listen to recognize someone's point of view • Listen to take notes **Pronunciation** • Pronunciation of unstressed vowels	**Texts** • A spa and fitness center advertisement • A health advice column • A photo story **Skills/strategies** • Paraphrase • Understand from context • Confirm content • Apply information	**Task** • Write a letter on how to improve appearance **WRITING BOOSTER** • Writing a formal letter

	COMMUNICATION GOALS	VOCABULARY	GRAMMAR
UNIT 6 Eating Well PAGE 62	• Talk about food passions • Make an excuse to decline food • Discuss lifestyle changes • Describe local dishes	• Nutrition terminology • Food passions • Excuses for not eating something • Food descriptions	• Use to / used to • Negative yes / no questions **GRAMMAR BOOSTER** • Use to / used to: use and form, common errors • Be used to vs. get used to • Repeated actions in the past: would + base form, common errors • Negative yes / no questions: short answers
UNIT 7 About Personality PAGE 74	• Get to know a new friend • Cheer someone up • Discuss personality and its origin • Examine the impact of birth order on personality	• Positive and negative adjectives • Terms to discuss psychology and personality	• Gerunds and infinitives • Gerunds as objects of prepositions **GRAMMAR BOOSTER** • Gerunds and infinitives: other uses • Negative gerunds

UNIT 8
The Arts
PAGE 86
	• Recommend a museum
	• Ask about and describe objects
	• Talk about artistic talent
	• Discuss your favorite artists
		• Kinds of art
		• Adjectives to describe art
		• Objects, handicrafts, and materials
		• Passive participial phrases
			• The passive voice
			  ○ Form, meaning, and usage
			  ○ Statements and questions
			
			GRAMMAR BOOSTER
			• Transitive and intransitive verbs
			• The passive voice: other tenses
			• Yes / no questions in the passive voice: other tenses

UNIT 9
Living in
Cyberspace
PAGE 98
	• Troubleshoot a problem
	• Compare product features
	• Describe how you use the Internet
	• Discuss the impact of the Internet
		• Ways to reassure someone
		• The computer screen, components, and commands
		• Internet activities
			• The infinitive of purpose
			• Comparisons with as . . . as
			  ○ Meaning and usage
			  ○ Just, almost, not quite, not nearly
			
			GRAMMAR BOOSTER
			• Expressing purpose with in order to and for
			• As . . . as to compare adverbs
			• Comparatives / superlatives: review
			• Comparison with adverbs

UNIT 10
Ethics and
Values
PAGE 110
	• Discuss ethical choices
	• Return someone else's property
	• Express personal values
	• Discuss acts of kindness and honesty
		• Idioms
		• Situations that require an ethical choice
		• Acknowledging thanks
		• Personal values
			• The unreal conditional
			  ○ Form, usage, common errors
			• Possessive pronouns / Whose
			  ○ Form, usage, common errors
			
			GRAMMAR BOOSTER
			• should, ought to, had better
			• have to, must, be supposed to
			• Possessive nouns: review and expansion
			• Pronouns: summary

CONVERSATION STRATEGIES	LISTENING / PRONUNCIATION	READING	WRITING
• Provide an emphatic affirmative response with "Definitely." • Offer food with "Please help yourself." • Acknowledge someone's efforts by saying something positive • Soften the rejection of an offer with "I'll pass on the ___." • Use a negative question to express surprise • Use "It's not a problem." to downplay inconvenience	**Listening Skills** • Listen for details • Listen to personalize **Pronunciation** • Sound reduction: <u>used to</u>	**Texts** • A food guide • Descriptions of types of diets • A magazine article about eating habits • A lifestyle survey • Menu ingredients • A photo story **Skills/strategies** • Understand from context • Summarize • Compare and contrast	**Task** • Write a persuasive paragraph about the differences in present-day and past diets **WRITING BOOSTER** • Connecting ideas: subordinating conjunctions
• Clarify an earlier question with "Well, for example, . . ." • Buy time to think with "Let's see." • Use auxiliary <u>do</u> to emphasize a verb • Thank someone for showing interest. • Offer empathy with "I know what you mean."	**Listening Skills** • Listen for main ideas • Listen for specific information • Classify information • Infer information **Pronunciation** • Reduction of <u>to</u> in infinitives	**Texts** • A pop psychology website • A textbook excerpt about the nature / nurture controversy • Personality surveys • A photo story **Skills/strategies** • Understand vocabulary from context • Make personal comparisons	**Task** • Write an essay describing someone's personality **WRITING BOOSTER** • Parallel structure
• Say "Be sure not to miss ___." to emphasize the importance of an action • Introduce the first aspect of an opinion with "For one thing, . . ." • Express enthusiasm for what someone has said with "No kidding!" • Invite someone's opinion with "What do you think of ___?"	**Listening Skills** • Understand from context • Listen to take notes • Infer point of view **Pronunciation** • Emphatic stress	**Texts** • Museum descriptions • A book excerpt about the origin of artistic talent • An artistic survey • A photo story **Skills/strategies** • Recognize the main idea • Identify supporting details • Paraphrase	**Task** • Write a detailed description of a decorative object **WRITING BOOSTER** • Providing supporting details
• Ask for assistance with "Could you take a look at ___?" • Introduce an explanation with "Well, . . ." • Make a suggestion with "Why don't you try ___ing?" • Express interest informally with "Oh, yeah?" • Use "Everyone says . . ." to introduce a popular opinion • Say "Well, I've heard ___." to support a point of view	**Listening Skills** • Listen for the main idea • Listen for details **Pronunciation** • Stress in <u>as</u> . . . <u>as</u> phrases	**Texts** • A social network website • An internet user survey • Newspaper clippings about the Internet • A photo story **Skills/strategies** • Understand from context • Relate to personal experience	**Task** • Write an essay evaluating the benefits and problems of the Internet **WRITING BOOSTER** • Organizing ideas
• Say "You think so?" to reconfirm someone's opinion • Provide an emphatic affirmative response with "Absolutely." • Acknowledge thanks with "Don't mention it."	**Listening Skills** • Listen to infer information • Listen for main ideas • Understand vocabulary from context • Support ideas with details **Pronunciation** • Blending of <u>d</u> + <u>y</u> in <u>would you</u>	**Texts** • A personal values self-test • Print and online news stories about kindness and honesty • A photo story **Skills/strategies** • Summarize • Interpret information • Relate to personal experience	**Task** • Write an essay about someone's personal choice **WRITING BOOSTER** • Introducing conflicting ideas: <u>On the one hand</u>; <u>On the other hand</u>

TO THE TEACHER

What is *Top Notch*?
Top Notch is a six-level* communicative course that prepares adults and young adults to interact successfully and confidently with both native and non-native speakers of English.

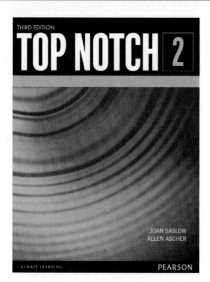

The goal of *Top Notch* is to make English unforgettable through:
- Multiple exposures to new language
- Numerous opportunities to practice it
- Deliberate and intensive recycling

The *Top Notch* course has two beginning levels—*Top Notch Fundamentals* for true beginners and *Top Notch 1* for false beginners. *Top Notch* is benchmarked to the Global Scale of English and is tightly correlated to the Can-do Statements of the Common European Framework of Reference.

Each full level of *Top Notch* contains material for 60–90 hours of classroom instruction. In addition, the entire course can be tailored to blended learning with an integrated online component, *MyEnglishLab*.

NEW This third edition of *Top Notch* includes these new features: Extra Grammar Exercises, digital full-color Vocabulary Flash Cards, Conversation Activator videos, and Pronunciation Coach videos.

* *Summit 1* and *Summit 2* are the titles of the 5th and 6th levels of the *Top Notch* course.

Award-Winning Instructional Design*

Daily confirmation of progress

Each easy-to-follow two-page lesson begins with a clearly stated practical communication goal closely aligned to the Common European Framework's Can-do Statements. All activities are integrated with the goal, giving vocabulary and grammar meaning and purpose. *Now You Can* activities ensure that students achieve each goal and confirm their progress in every class session.

Explicit vocabulary and grammar

Clear captioned picture-dictionary illustrations with accompanying audio take the guesswork out of meaning and pronunciation. Grammar presentations containing both rules and examples clarify form, meaning, and use. The unique *Recycle this Language* feature continually puts known words and grammar in front of students' eyes as they communicate, to make sure language remains active.

High-frequency social language

Twenty memorable conversation models provide appealing natural social language that students can carry "in their pockets" for use in real life. Rigorous controlled and free discussion activities systematically stimulate recycling of social language, ensuring that it's not forgotten.

Linguistic and cultural fluency

Top Notch equips students to interact with people from different language backgrounds by including authentic accents on the audio. Conversation Models, Photo Stories, and cultural fluency activities prepare students for social interactions in English with people from unfamiliar cultures.

Active listening syllabus

All Vocabulary presentations, Pronunciation presentations, Conversation Models, Photo Stories, Listening Comprehension exercises, and Readings are recorded on the audio to help students develop good pronunciation, intonation, and auditory memory. In addition, approximately fifty carefully developed listening tasks at each level of *Top Notch* develop crucial listening comprehension skills such as listen for details, listen for main ideas, listen to activate vocabulary, listen to activate grammar, and listen to confirm information.

*We wish you and your students enjoyment and success with **Top Notch 2**. We wrote it for you.*

Joan Saslow and Allen Ascher

* *Top Notch* is the recipient of the Association of Educational Publishers' *Distinguished Achievement Award*.

ActiveTeach

Maximize the impact of your *Top Notch* lessons. This digital tool provides an interactive classroom experience that can be used with or without an interactive whiteboard (IWB). It includes a full array of digital and printable features.

For class presentation . . .

- 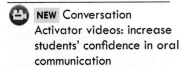 **NEW** Conversation Activator videos: increase students' confidence in oral communication

- 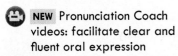 **NEW** Pronunciation Coach videos: facilitate clear and fluent oral expression

- 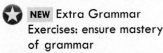 **NEW** Extra Grammar Exercises: ensure mastery of grammar

- **V** **NEW** Digital Full-Color Vocabulary Flash Cards: accelerate retention of new vocabulary

PLUS

- ▶ Clickable Audio: instant access to the complete classroom audio program
- *Top Notch TV* Video Program: a hilarious sitcom and authentic on-the-street interviews
- *Top Notch Pop* Songs and Karaoke: original songs for additional language practice

For planning . . .

- A *Methods Handbook* for a communicative classroom
- Detailed timed lesson plans for each two-page lesson
- *Top Notch TV* teaching notes
- Complete answer keys, audio scripts, and video scripts

For extra support . . .

- Hundreds of extra printable activities, with teaching notes
- *Top Notch Pop* language exercises
- *Top Notch TV* activity worksheets

For assessment . . .

- Ready-made unit and review achievement tests with options to edit, add, or delete items.

MyEnglishLab

An optional online learning tool

- **NEW** Grammar Coach videos, plus the Pronunciation Coach videos, and Digital Vocabulary Flash Cards
- **NEW** Immediate and meaningful feedback on wrong answers
- **NEW** Remedial grammar exercises
- Interactive practice of all material presented in the course
- Grade reports that display performance and time on task
- Auto-graded achievement tests

Workbook

Lesson-by-lesson written exercises to accompany the Student's Book

Full-Course Placement Tests

Choose printable or online version

Classroom Audio Program

- A set of Audio CDs, as an alternative to the clickable audio in the ActiveTeach
- Contains a variety of authentic regional and non-native accents to build comprehension of diverse English speakers
- **NEW** The entire audio program is available for students at www.english.com/topnotch3e. The mobile app *Top Notch Go* allows access anytime, anywhere and lets students practice at their own pace.

Teacher's Edition and Lesson Planner

- Detailed interleaved lesson plans, language and culture notes, answer keys, and more
- Also accessible in digital form in the ActiveTeach

Grammar Readiness
SELF-CHECK

The Grammar Readiness Self-Check is optional. Complete the exercises to confirm that you know this grammar previously taught in _Top Notch_.

THE SIMPLE PRESENT TENSE AND THE PRESENT CONTINUOUS

A   PRACTICE Choose the correct verb or verb phrase.

1 We (take / <u>are taking</u>) a trip to California this weekend.

2 The flight (arrives / <u>is arriving</u>) now. That's great because the flights in this airport usually (<u>arrive</u> / are arriving) late.

3 Please drive slower! You (go / are going) too fast!

4 (<u>Does it rain</u> / Is it raining) often in March?

5 Brandon (goes / <u>is going</u>) skiing on his next vacation.

6 We (<u>like</u> / are liking) milk in both coffee and tea.

B   USE THE GRAMMAR Complete each statement with the simple present tense or the present continuous.

1 In my family, we usually ....

2 Next weekend, I ....

BE GOING TO + BASE FORM FOR THE FUTURE

A   PRACTICE Complete the conversations with <u>be going to</u>. Use contractions.

1 **A:** What .... (they / do) after English class?
  B: They .... (go) out to eat.

2 **A:** I .... (need) a rental car in Chicago.
  B: .... (you / make) a reservation online?

3 **A:** Who .... (you / call) when your plane lands?
  B: My wife. She .... (wait) for my call in the airport café.

4 **A:** What .... (you / do) when you get to New York?
  B: The first thing .... (we / do) is eat!

5 **A:** Who .... (be) at the meeting?
  B: My colleagues from the office. And my boss .... (come), too.

B   USE THE GRAMMAR Write your own question and answer, using <u>be going to</u> + a base form.

Q: ....

....

A: ....

....

CAN, HAVE TO, COULD, AND SHOULD: MEANING AND FORM

A PRACTICE Choose the correct phrases.

1 We .... a reservation if we want a good room.
   a couldn't make   **b** should make   **c** should making

2 Susan doesn't have to wear formal clothes to the office. She .... jeans.
   a can't wear   **b** can wearing   **c** can wear

3 Dan can't go shopping this afternoon. He .... drive his children to school.
   a have to   **b** has to   **c** doesn't have to

4 They just missed the 3:12 express bus, but they .... the 3:14 local because it arrives too late. They should take a taxi.
   a could take   **b** shouldn't to take   **c** shouldn't take

5 The class has to end on time so the students .... the bus to the party.
   a can take   **b** can to take   **c** can't take

6 I can sleep late tomorrow. I .... go to the office.
   a have to   **b** don't have to   **c** doesn't have to

B USE THE GRAMMAR Write one statement with both <u>can</u> and <u>have to</u>. Write one statement with either <u>should</u> or <u>could</u>.

1 ....

2 ....

OBJECT PRONOUNS

A PRACTICE Rewrite each sentence, correcting the error.

1 Please call about it us. ....

2 She's buying for you it. ....

3 The brown shoes? She doesn't like on him them. ....

4 He wrote for her it. ....

5 They're giving to them it. ....

B USE THE GRAMMAR Rewrite each sentence, changing the two nouns to object pronouns.

1 I gave my sister the present yesterday. ....

2 The clerk gift-wrapped the sweaters for John. ....

COMPARATIVE ADJECTIVES

A PRACTICE Complete each sentence with the comparative form of the adjective.

1 I think very cold weather is .... (bad) than very hot weather.

2 A tablet is .... (convenient) than a laptop.

3 A T-shirt is .... (comfortable) than a sweatshirt in hot weather.

4 The clothes in a department store are usually .... (affordable) than ones in a small neighborhood store.

5 Orange juice is .... (good) for your health than orange soda.

6 Rio is pretty hot in the summer, but Salvador is .... (hot).

7 If you're getting dressed for the office, you should wear a .... (long) skirt.

B   USE THE GRAMMAR Write your own two sentences, using one of these adjectives in comparative form in each sentence: <u>cheap</u>, <u>popular</u>, <u>near</u>, <u>fast</u>.

1 ....

2 ....

SUPERLATIVE ADJECTIVES

A   PRACTICE Write statements with the superlative form of each adjective.

1 old *The oldest person in the world is 124 years old.* ....

2 good ....

3 funny ....

4 appropriate ....

5 unusual ....

6 large ....

7 beautiful ....

8 short ....

9 interesting ....

10 crazy ....

B   USE THE GRAMMAR Write one statement about yourself, using a superlative adjective.

....

THE SIMPLE PAST TENSE: STATEMENTS

A   PRACTICE Complete the paragraph with the simple past tense.

Chris .... (1 go) to New York at the end of the school year. His flight .... (2 get in) late, so he .... (3 take) a taxi directly to his hotel and .... (4 eat) something fast at the hotel café. Chris .... (5 have) tickets to a Broadway show, and he .... (6 not have) time to eat at a regular restaurant. Just before the show, he .... (7 meet) his friends in front of the theater. He really .... (8 love) the show. After the show, he .... (9 buy) a book about it. His friends .... (10 say) good night, and Chris .... (11 walk) back to the hotel, ... (12 drink) a big glass of cold juice, ... (13 go) to bed, and .... (14 sleep) for 10 hours.

B **USE THE GRAMMAR** Write four statements about what you did yesterday. Use one of these verbs in each statement: go, get dressed, eat, come home

1 ....

2 ....

3 ....

4 ....

THE SIMPLE PAST TENSE: YES / NO QUESTIONS

A **PRACTICE** Change each statement to a yes / no question.

1 Phil lost his luggage on the flight. ....

2 They drove too fast. ....

3 She wrote a letter to her uncle. ....

4 They found a wallet on the street. ....

5 Claire's husband spent a lot of money at the mall. ....

6 Ms. Carter taught her children to play the piano. ....

B **USE THE GRAMMAR** Write three yes / no questions. Use each of these verbs: bring, speak, break.

1 ....

2 ....

3 ....

THE SIMPLE PAST TENSE: INFORMATION QUESTIONS

A **PRACTICE** Complete each conversation with an information question in the simple past tense.

1 **A:** .... Chinese?
  B: I studied in Shanghai.

2 **A:** .... your husband?
  B: I met him two years ago.

3 **A:** .... about the problem?
  B: I called my daughter. She always knows what to do.

4 **A:** .... your car?
  B: My brother-in-law bought it. He needed a new car.

5 **A:** .... in Mexico?
  B: My parents lived there for more than ten years.

B **USE THE GRAMMAR** Write two information questions in the simple past tense, one with How and one with What.

1 ....

2 ....

COMMUNICATION GOALS
1 Get reacquainted with someone.
2 Greet a visitor to your country.
3 Discuss gestures and customs.
4 Describe an interesting experience.

PREVIEW

CUSTOMS AROUND THE WORLD

Greetings
People greet each other differently around the world.

Some people bow. | **Some people kiss once. Some kiss twice.** | **Some shake hands.** | **And some hug.**

Exchanging Business Cards

People have different customs for exchanging business cards around the world.

Some customs are very formal. People always use two hands and look at the card carefully. | **Other customs are informal. People accept a card with one hand and quickly put it in a pocket.**

Getting Acquainted

What about small talk—the topics people talk about when they don't know each other well?

In some places, it's not polite to ask people about how much money they make or how old they are. But in other places, people think those topics are appropriate.

A **PAIR WORK** In your opinion, is there a right way and a wrong way to greet people? Explain.

B **DISCUSSION** In your country, are there any topics people should avoid during small talk? What about the topics below?

- the weather
- someone's job
- someone's religion
- someone's family
- someone's home
- (other) ___

C   ▶1:02 **PHOTO STORY**   Read and listen to two people meeting in a hotel lobby.

ENGLISH FOR TODAY'S WORLD
Understand English speakers from
different language backgrounds.
Leon = Spanish speaker
Taka = Japanese speaker

Leon: You look familiar. Haven't we met somewhere before?

Taka: I don't think so. I'm not from around here.

Leon: I know! Aren't you from Japan? I'm sure we met at the IT conference last week.

Taka: Of course! You're from Mexico, right?

Leon: That's right. I'm sorry. I've forgotten your name.

Taka: Kamura Takashi. But you can call me Taka.

Leon: Hi, Taka. Leon Prieto. Please call me Leon. So, what have you been up to since the conference?

Taka: Not much. Actually, I'm on my way to the airport now. I'm flying back home.

Leon: Hey, we should keep in touch. Here's my card. The conference is in Acapulco next year and I could show you around.

Taka: That would be great. I hear Acapulco's beautiful.

Leon: It was nice to see you again, Taka.

Taka: You, too.

D   **FOCUS ON LANGUAGE**   Find the underlined expression in the Photo Story that matches each explanation.

1 You say this when you want to offer to introduce someone to a new place.   *I could*

2 You say this to suggest that someone call or e-mail you in the future.   *We should.*

3 You say this when you're not sure if you know someone, but you think you might.   *You look familiar.*

4 You say this when you want to ask about someone's recent activities.   *what have you been -*

E   **THINK AND EXPLAIN**   Answer the questions, according to the Photo Story. Explain your answers.

1 Why does Leon begin speaking with Taka?

2 Has Taka been busy since the conference?

> Because he thinks he knows Taka. He says, 'You look familiar.'

3 Why does Leon give Taka his business card?   *he wants to keep in touch.*

4 What does Leon offer to do at the next conference?   *I could show you around.*

SPEAKING

PAIR WORK   With a partner, discuss and write advice for visitors about how to behave in your country. Then share your advice with the class.

> Questions like *How old are you?* and *How much money do you make?* aren't polite. You shouldn't ask them.

> Don't exchange business cards with one hand! Always use two hands.

Your advice
1
2
3

GOAL Get reacquainted with someone

GRAMMAR *The present perfect*

Use the present perfect to talk about an indefinite time in the past.
Form the present perfect with <u>have</u> or <u>has</u> and a past participle.

Affirmative and negative statements

We	've haven't	met them.

She	's hasn't	called him.

<u>Yes</u> / <u>no</u> questions

A: **Have** you **met** them?
B: Yes, we **have**. / No, we **haven't**.

A: **Has** she **called** him?
B: Yes, she **has**. / No, she **hasn't**.

Remember: Use the simple past tense to talk about a definite or specific time.

present perfect: indefinite time	simple past tense: definite time
I've met Bill twice.	We met in 1999 and again in 2004.

Contractions

've met = have met	's met = has met
haven't met = have not met	hasn't met = has not met

For regular verbs, the past participle form is the same as the simple past form.
open → opened
study → studied

Irregular verbs

base form	simple past	past participle
be	was / were	**been**
come	came	**come**
do	did	**done**
eat	ate	**eaten**
fall	fell	**fallen**
go	went	**gone**
have	had	**had**
make	made	**made**
meet	met	**met**
see	saw	**seen**
speak	spoke	**spoken**
take	took	**taken**
write	wrote	**written**

For more irregular verb forms, see page 123.

GRAMMAR BOOSTER p. 126
• The present perfect: information questions

A Choose the correct form to complete each sentence.

1 We've .... the 2:00 express train many times.
   a take   **b** took   **c** taken

2 I had breakfast at 9:00, but I haven't .... lunch.
   a have   **b** had   **c** having

3 Alison has .... to the mall.
   a went   **b** gone   **c** go

4 My younger brother has .... home from work.
   a come   **b** came   **c** comes

5 They posted some messages yesterday, but they haven't .... anything about their trip.
   a written   **b** write   **c** wrote

B **PAIR WORK** Complete the conversations with the present perfect or the simple past tense. Then practice the conversations with a partner.

1 A: .... our new teacher?
      Jake / meet
   B: Yes, ... He .... her in the office this morning.
                                              meet

2 A: .... to this class before?
      they / be
   B: No, ... They're new at this school.

3 A: .... in the new school restaurant?
         you / eat
   B: No, ... Is it good?

4 A: .... with the school director?
      your classmates / speak
   B: Yes, ... They .... with her yesterday.
                                              speak

5 A: .... the new language lab?
         Beth / see
   B: No, ... But she .... the library.
                                              see

C **GRAMMAR PRACTICE** Complete the message with the present perfect or the simple past tense.

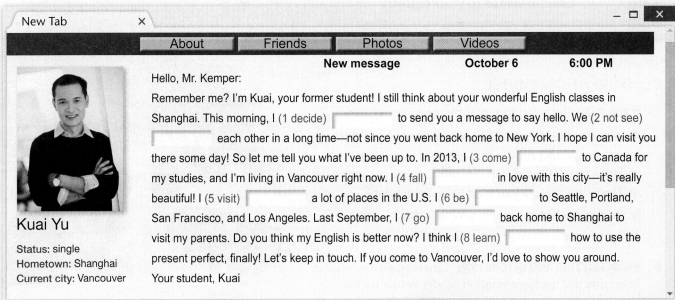

New Tab   ✕

About   Friends   Photos   Videos

New message   October 6   6:00 PM

Hello, Mr. Kemper:

Remember me? I'm Kuai, your former student! I still think about your wonderful English classes in Shanghai. This morning, I (1 decide) [_____] to send you a message to say hello. We (2 not see) [_____] each other in a long time—not since you went back home to New York. I hope I can visit you there some day! So let me tell you what I've been up to. In 2013, I (3 come) [_____] to Canada for my studies, and I'm living in Vancouver right now. I (4 fall) [_____] in love with this city—it's really beautiful! I (5 visit) [_____] a lot of places in the U.S. I (6 be) [_____] to Seattle, Portland, San Francisco, and Los Angeles. Last September, I (7 go) [_____] back home to Shanghai to visit my parents. Do you think my English is better now? I think I (8 learn) [_____] how to use the present perfect, finally! Let's keep in touch. If you come to Vancouver, I'd love to show you around.

Your student, Kuai

Kuai Yu

Status: single
Hometown: Shanghai
Current city: Vancouver

DIGITAL
MORE
EXERCISES

CONVERSATION MODEL

A ▶1:03 Read and listen to people getting reacquainted.

A: Audrey, have you met Hanah?

B: No, I haven't.

A: Hanah, I'd like you to meet Audrey.

C: Hi, Audrey. You look familiar. Have we met before?

B: I don't think so.

C: I know! Last month. You were at my sister Nicole's party.

B: Oh, that's right! How have you been?

B ▶1:04 **RHYTHM AND INTONATION** Listen again and repeat. Then practice the Conversation Model with a partner.

DIGITAL
VIDEO
COACH

PRONUNCIATION *Sound reduction in the present perfect*

A ▶1:05 Listen to how the sound /t/ of the negative contraction "disappears" in natural speech. Then listen again and repeat.

1 I haven't been to that class.   **3** They haven't taken the test.

2 He hasn't met his new teacher.   **4** She hasn't heard the news.

B Now practice saying the sentences on your own.

NOW YOU CAN Get reacquainted with someone

DIGITAL
VIDEO **CONVERSATION ACTIVATOR** With two other students, practice making introductions and getting reacquainted. Use your own names and the present perfect. Then change roles.

A: .... , have you met .... ?
B: No, I haven't.
A: .... , I'd like you to meet ....
C: .... You look familiar. Have we met before?
B: ....

DON'T STOP!
• Say how you have been.
• Say more about the time you met.
• Introduce other classmates.

Ideas
You met ...
• at a party
• at a meeting
• at a friend's house
• in another class
• (your own idea) ___

GOAL Greet a visitor to your country

The Forbidden Palace

CONVERSATION MODEL

A ▶1:06 Read and listen to someone greeting a visitor.

A: Welcome to Beijing. Have you ever been here before?

B: No, it's my first time. But yesterday I went to the Forbidden Palace. It was fantastic!

A: That's great. Have you tried Beijing duck yet?

B: Beijing duck? No, I haven't. What's that?

A: It's a famous Chinese dish. I think you'll like it.

B ▶1:07 **RHYTHM AND INTONATION** Listen again and repeat. Then practice the Conversation Model with a partner.

Beijing duck

VOCABULARY *Tourist activities around the world*

A ▶1:08 Read and listen. Then listen again and repeat.

climb Mt. Fuji

go sightseeing in New York

go to the top of the Eiffel Tower

try Korean food

take a tour of the Tower of London

take pictures of the Great Wall

B **PAIR WORK** Use the Vocabulary to say what you have and haven't done.

❝ I've climbed two famous mountains. ❞

❝ I haven't tried Indian food. ❞

GRAMMAR *The present perfect: already, yet, ever, before, and never*

Use ever or before in yes / no questions about *life experiences*.

Have you **ever** eaten Indian food?   Has he been to Paris **before**?

Use yet or already in yes / no questions about *recent experiences*.

Have you toured Quito **yet**?   Has she **already** been to the top of the Eiffel Tower?

In affirmative and negative statements

We've **already** seen the Great Wall.   We haven't tried Beijing duck **yet**.
They have **never** visited Mexico.   They haven't **ever** visited Mexico.
He's been to New York **before**.   He hasn't been to Boston **before**.

Always place **before** and **yet** at the end of statements and questions.

Be careful!

I **have never** (OR **haven't ever**) been there.
NOT I ~~haven't never~~ been there.

GRAMMAR BOOSTER p. 126
• Yet and already: expansion, common errors
• Ever, never, and before: use and placement

A **GRAMMAR PRACTICE**   Use the words to write statements or questions in the present perfect.

1 (you / go sightseeing / in London / before)
2 (she / already / try / Guatemalan food)
3 (they / ever / be / to Buenos Aires)
4 (we / not take a tour of / Prague / yet)

B ▶ 1:09 **LISTEN TO ACTIVATE GRAMMAR**   Listen and complete the questions, using the Vocabulary. Then listen again and complete the short answers.

Questions

1 Has she .... of the Taj Mahal yet?
2 Has he .... in Kyoto yet?
3 Has she ever .... ceviche?
4 Has he already .... the Pyramid of the Sun?
5 Has she ever .... to Rio de Janeiro before?
6 Has she .... of Sugarloaf yet?

Short Answers

.... , she ....
.... , he ....
.... , she ....
.... , he ....
.... , she ....
.... , she ....

The Taj Mahal • India

A temple • Kyoto, Japan

Ceviche • Peru

The Pyramid of the Sun • Mexico City

Sugarloaf • Rio de Janeiro, Brazil

C Write five questions about tourist activities in your city or country. Use <u>yet</u>, <u>already</u>, <u>ever</u>, and <u>before</u>.

Have you ever tried our seafood dishes?

1 ....
2 ....
3 ....
4 ....
5 ....

DIGITAL
MORE
EXERCISES

NOW YOU CAN Greet a visitor to your country

A **NOTEPADDING**   On the notepad, write at least five activities for a tourist in your city or country.

DIGITAL
VIDEO

B **CONVERSATION ACTIVATOR**   With a partner, change the Conversation Model to greet a visitor to <u>your</u> country. Use the present perfect. Suggest tourist activities in your city. Use your notepad. Then change roles.

A: Welcome to .... Have you ever been here before?
B: No, it's my first time. But yesterday I ....
A: .... Have you .... yet?
B: .... **DON'T STOP!**

• Ask about other places and tourist activities.

Activity	Description
try Beijing duck	It's a famous Chinese dish.

Activity	Description

C **CHANGE PARTNERS**   Practice the conversation again, asking about other tourist activities on your notepad.

BEFORE YOU READ

▶1:10 **VOCABULARY • *The hand*** Read and listen.
Then listen again and repeat.

1 thumb
2 index finger
3 middle finger
4 ring finger
5 pinkie
6 palm
7 fist

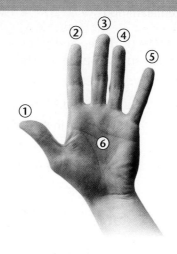

READING ▶1:11

We talked to June Galloway about her book,
Get off on the Right Foot: Don't Let the Wrong Gesture Ruin Your Day.

English is the world's international language. But in your book, you've focused on non-verbal communication. Why is that so important?
Well, gestures and other body language can have different meanings in different places. Something that you think is friendly or polite could come across as very rude in another culture. I've described many of these customs and cultural differences so my readers don't get off on the wrong foot when they meet people from places where the culture differs from their own.

Can greeting someone in the wrong way really lead to misunderstanding?
In some cases, yes. The firm handshake a North American expects may seem quite aggressive in other places. And a light handshake—which is normal in some countries—may seem unfriendly to a North American.

In what ways can hand gestures lead to misunderstanding?
Well, as an example, we assume all people indicate the numbers one to ten with their fingers the same way. But in fact, they don't. While North Americans usually use an index finger for "one," most Europeans use a thumb. North Americans extend all ten fingers for "ten." However, Chinese indicate the numbers one to ten all on one hand. For example, an extended thumb and pinkie means "six," and a fist means "ten." Imagine how confusing this can be when you're trying to communicate quantities and prices with your hands!

What other gestures can cause confusion?
Take the gesture for "come here," for example. In North America, people gesture with the palm up. Well, in southern Europe, that gesture means "good-bye"! And in many Asian countries, the palm-up gesture is considered rude. Instead, people there gesture with the palm down.

I've heard that, in Japan, pointing with the index finger is not polite. Is that right?
Yes. Japanese prefer to point with the palm open and facing up.

Surely there must be some gestures used everywhere, right? What about the thumbs-up sign for "great"?
Sorry. That's extremely rude in Australia and the Middle East. This is why it's so important to be aware of these cultural differences.

What gesture do you use . . .

. . . for the number six?

. . . for "Come here": palm up or down?

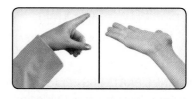

. . . for pointing? Do you use your index finger or an open palm?

A **IDENTIFY SUPPORTING DETAILS** Check the statements that are true, according to the article. Write X next to the statements that are not true. Explain your answers.

- ☐ 1 In most of Europe, a thumb and an index finger mean "two."
- ☐ 2 In North America, a thumb and a pinkie mean "two."
- ☐ 3 Japanese point at pictures with an open palm facing up.
- ☐ 4 To be friendly, North Americans greet others with a light handshake.
- ☐ 5 Everyone uses the thumbs-up sign for "that's good."

> ❝ True. Galloway says most Europeans begin with the thumb. So the index finger is the next finger after that. ❞

B **RELATE TO PERSONAL EXPERIENCE** Discuss the questions.

DIGITAL MORE RCISES

Have you ever been surprised by someone's gestures or body language on TV, in the movies, or in real life? What did you see? What do you think the action meant? Why were you surprised?

NOW YOU CAN Discuss gestures and customs

A **PAIR WORK** Read the travel tips about gestures and customs around the world. Compare your own gestures and customs with those described. Do any of them seem strange or rude?

Travel Tips ✈

If someone gives you a gift, thank the person and open it right away. (Ecuador)	**When a visitor is leaving your home,** you should walk with that person out the door. (Korea)	**If you are going to be more than 15 minutes late for a party, lunch, or dinner,** you should call to explain. (United States)	**To gesture that something is good,** hold your hand up, palm facing out, and slowly bring all your fingers to the thumb. (Turkey)
If you want to get a server's attention, it's more polite to use eye contact rather than hand gestures. (Kenya)	**When greeting people,** older people should always be greeted first. (Mongolia)	**Before you enter someone's home,** you should take off your shoes. (Ukraine)	

B **NOTEPADDING** With a partner, choose a topic and discuss your country's customs. Then write notes about your country on the notepad.

> Topic: *showing respect for older people.*
> Customs: *It's not polite to disagree with an older person.*

Topic:
Customs:
Are the rules the same for both men and women? How about for young people or older people? Explain.

Topics
- showing respect to older people
- do's and don'ts for gestures
- topics for polite small talk
- invitations
- visiting someone's home
- giving gifts
- offering or refusing food
- touching or not touching
- (your own topic) ___

Text-mining (optional)
Find and underline three words or phrases in the Reading that were new to you. Use them in your Discussion.
For example: "body language."

C **DISCUSSION** Tell your classmates about the customs you described on your notepad. Does everyone agree?

GOAL Describe an interesting experience

BEFORE YOU LISTEN

A ▶1:12 **VOCABULARY • *Participial adjectives*** Read and listen. Then listen again and repeat.

The safari was **fascinating**.
(They were **fascinated**.)

The ski trip was **thrilling**.
(They were **thrilled**.)

The sky-dive was **frightening**.
(They were **frightened**.)

The food was **disgusting**.
(They were **disgusted**.)

B Write lists of things you think are fascinating, thrilling, frightening, or disgusting.

C **PAIR WORK** Compare your lists.

" I've never eaten snails. I think they're disgusting! "

" Really? I've tried them, and I wasn't disgusted at all. They're good! "

LISTENING COMPREHENSION

A ▶1:13 **LISTEN TO CLASSIFY** Listen to the three interviews. Then listen again and write the number of the speaker described by each statement.

....3.... **a** travels to have thrilling experiences

.... **b** describes differences in body language

.... **c** was disgusted by something

.... **d** is fascinated by other cultures

.... **e** tries to be polite

.... **f** does things that other people think are frightening

Andrew Barlow

Nancy Sullivan

Mieko Nakamura

B ▶1:14 **LISTEN FOR DETAILS** Listen again and answer the questions in complete sentences.

1 Nancy Sullivan
   a How many countries has she visited? ....
   b What did she notice about gestures in India? ....

2 Andrew Barlow
   c What did the people in the village do to thank him? ....
   d Why did he eat something he didn't want to? ....

3 Mieko Nakamura
   e What has she done twice? ....
   f How did she get to "the top of the world"? ....

NOW YOU CAN Describe an interesting experience

A **NOTEPADDING** Answer the questions. Explain what happened. Write as many details as you can.

Have you ever been someplace that was really fascinating?
Have you ever eaten something that was really strange or disgusting?
Have you ever done something that was really thrilling or frightening?

B **PAIR WORK** Ask your partner about the experiences on his or her notepad.

DON'T STOP!
- Ask more questions.
- Ask about other experiences: "Have you ever . . ."

RECYCLE THIS LANGUAGE.
climb [a mountain]
go sightseeing in [Italy]
go to the top of [the Eiffel Tower]
try [snails]
take a tour of [New York]
take pictures of [the Taj Mahal]

C **GROUP WORK** Choose one of the experiences your partner told you about. Tell your classmates about your partner's experience.

❝ My partner went hang gliding last year. She was frightened, but it was really thrilling. ❞

hang gliding

REVIEW

A ▶1:15 Listen to the conversation with a tourist in Vancouver and check Yes or No. Then listen again and write the answers to the questions, using yet or already.

Has she. . .	Yes	No	
1 been to the Vancouver Aquarium?	☑	☐	*Yes. She's already been to the aquarium.*
2 visited Gastown?	☐	☐	....
3 been to the top of Grouse Mountain?	☐	☐	....
4 seen the Capilano Suspension Bridge?	☐	☐	....
5 tried dim sum?	☐	☐	....
6 gone to the top of the Harbour Centre Tower?	☐	☐	....

B Use the photos to write questions using the present perfect with ever or before. Don't use the same verb more than once.

Brazilian barbecue

Mount Fuji, Japan

Oriental Pearl Tower, Shanghai, China

Venice, Italy

1 .... 3 ....
2 .... 4 ....

C Write sentences about the topics. Use the present perfect.

1 *I've been to the top of the Taipei 101 Building.*

1 tall buildings you've been to the top of
2 cities or countries you've visited
3 foods you've tried
4 mountains or high places you've climbed

WRITING

Write about one of the interesting experiences you talked about in Lesson 4. Describe what happened, where you were, who you were with, and how you felt.

I've had a few frightening experiences in my life.
Last year, I was on vacation in . . .

For additional language practice . . .

♫ TOP NOTCH POP • Lyrics p. 153
"Greetings and Small Talk"
DIGITAL SONG   DIGITAL KARAOKE

WRITING BOOSTER p. 143
• Avoiding run-on sentences
• Guidance for this writing exercise

ORAL REVIEW

PAIR WORK

1 Create a conversation for the man and woman in photo 1.
  Imagine the man is welcoming the woman to his city.
  Choose one of the cities in the travel brochure.

  Welcome to Paris. Have you been here before?

2 Create a conversation for the three people in photo 2.
  Imagine they get reacquainted during a tour of Europe.

  A: *Have you met __?*
  B: *Actually, you look familiar. Have we met before?*
  C: *Yes, I think we have. We were at the …*

3 Look at the brochure and imagine that you are on one
  of these tours. Ask and answer questions, using the
  present perfect.

  Have you tried tapas yet?

Tour Europe

| SPAIN | FRANCE | ITALY | THE U.K. | RUSSIA |

Madrid, Spain

The Prado Museum

Tapas

Paris, France

The Eiffel Tower

Tour boat on the Seine River

Rome, Italy

The Colosseum

Gelato

London, the U.K.

The Millennium Wheel

Carnaby Street

Moscow, Russia

Borscht

Ballet at the Bolshoi Theater

✓ NOW I CAN

- ☐ Get reacquainted with someone.
- ☐ Greet a visitor to my country.
- ☐ Discuss gestures and customs.
- ☐ Describe an interesting experience.

Going to the Movies

COMMUNICATION GOALS
1 Apologize for being late.
2 Discuss preferences for movie genres.
3 Describe and recommend movies.
4 Discuss effects of violence on viewers.

PREVIEW

Log In | Your account | Help

WebFlicks   Stream to watch instantly or add disc to your wish list

Leonardo DiCaprio   Click on ▶ to preview movies.

Titanic 3D   1997 (3D 2012)
194 minutes
This 1997 blockbuster disaster movie
(11 Oscars!) is the true story of the
ill-fated ocean liner *Titanic*. But it's also
a 194-minute love story. Rose (Kate
Winslet), an unhappy young woman,
falls in love with Jack (DiCaprio), a poor
artist who gives her life meaning. The
scenes of the sinking of the magnificent
Titanic are truly frightening. An epic
classic romance!
Genre: Romantic drama, disaster

Blood Diamond   2006
143 minutes
DiCaprio stars as an ex-criminal
involved in the violent diamond trade
during the 1999 civil war in Sierra
Leone. He joins up with a fisherman
(Djimon Hounsou) to try to find a pink
diamond that they think can change
both of their lives. This thrilling action
movie will keep you sitting on the
edge of your seat.
Genre: Action, drama

The Great Gatsby   2013
143 minutes
This beautiful adaptation of
F. Scott Fitzgerald's fascinating 1925
novel of the same name tells the
story of neighbors from the fictional
town of West Egg on New York's Long
Island in the summer of 1922. The
main character, a mysterious
millionaire, Jay Gatsby (DiCaprio),
falls in love with the beautiful Daisy
Buchanan (Carey Mulligan), but the
story ends in tragedy.
Genre: Romantic drama

★★★★★   ★★★★⯪   ★★★★★

Stream	Stream	Stream
Add disc to your wish list	Add disc to your wish list	Add disc to your wish list

More DiCaprio movies

BY GENRE   **BY TITLE**
comedy   crime   The Man in the Iron Mask (1998)   The Aviator (2004)   Shutter Island (2010)
drama   romance   The Beach (2000)   The Departed (2006)   Inception (2010)
action   disaster   Gangs of New York (2002)   Body of Lies (2008)   The Wolf of Wall Street (2013)
                       Catch Me If You Can (2002)

A **PAIR WORK**   Did you see any of these DiCaprio movies when they were in the theater? If so,
tell your partner about them. If not, is there one you would like to see now? Explain why.

B **DISCUSSION**   Where do you like to see movies: at home or in a movie theater? Explain your reasons.

▶1:18 **PHOTO STORY** Read and listen to a conversation at a movie theater.

Anna: So, what are you in the mood for? They've got a bunch of great classic movies tonight.

Peter: They sure do. Hey, you're a big DiCaprio fan. I missed *Gangs of New York* when it was playing. Have you ever seen it?

Anna: Nope, I haven't. I've heard it's pretty violent. Frankly, I just can't take all that fighting.

Peter: Yeah. It *is* supposed to be pretty bloody. . . . What else?

Anna: Well, there's *Ice Age*. They say it's spectacular. What do you think?

Peter: Hmm. To tell you the truth, I can't stand animated films. Sorry. I've just never liked them. I think I'd rather see something . . .

Peter: Hey! What about *Casablanca*?

Anna: *Casablanca*? Now you're talking! And by the way, it's my treat. You paid last time. What do you say?

Peter: It's a deal! I'll get the popcorn.

D **FOCUS ON LANGUAGE** Find underlined words or phrases in the Photo Story that have almost the same meaning as the ones below.

1 "I'll pay."
2 "really don't like"
3 "To tell you the truth, . . ."
4 "a lot of"
5 "I didn't see . . ."
6 "They say . . ."

E **INFER MEANING** With a partner, discuss, find, and underline . . .

1 a noun that has the same meaning as "movie."
2 two different adjectives that are related to "fighting" or "killing."
3 an adjective that means "really great."

F **THINK AND EXPLAIN** First answer each question. Then explain your answer with a quotation from the Photo Story.

1 What actor does Anna like? _Leonardo DiCaprio_
   How do you know?
   Peter says, "Hey, you're a big DiCaprio fan."

2 Did Anna see *Gangs of New York*? ....
   How do you know?
   ....

3 What movie does Anna suggest? ....
   How do you know?
   ....

4 Who is going to pay for the popcorn? ....
   How do you know?
   ....

SPEAKING

PAIR WORK Make a list of movies playing in your town. Which movies would you like to see? Which movies would you not like to see? Give reasons for your answers.

GOAL Apologize for being late

GRAMMAR *The present perfect: for and since; Other uses of the present perfect*

Use <u>for</u> and <u>since</u> to describe periods of time that began in the past. Use <u>for</u> to describe a length of time. Use <u>since</u> with a specific time or date in the past.

How long have you been here?
- I've been here **for ten minutes.** (a length of time)
- I've been here **for many years.** (a length of time)
- I've been here **since eight o'clock.** (a specific time in the past)

> **Be careful!**
> They've lived here since **2013**.
> NOT They've lived here since ~~five years~~.

Other uses:

- with <u>always</u>: I've **always** wanted to see *Car Planet*.
- with ordinals and superlatives: This is **the third time** I've seen *Ping Pong*. It's **the best** movie I've ever seen.

- with <u>lately</u>, <u>recently</u>, or <u>just</u>: Have you seen a good movie **recently (or lately)**? I've **just** seen *The Beach*—what a great movie!
- with <u>still</u> or <u>so far</u>: You **still** haven't seen *Tomato Babies*? I've seen it three times **so far**!

> **GRAMMAR BOOSTER** p. 127
> - The present perfect continuous: unfinished actions
> - Spelling rules for the present participle: review, common errors

A **GRAMMAR PRACTICE** Choose the correct words to complete the paragraph.

I've been a big fan of Penélope Cruz (1 for / since) more than twenty years. I've followed her career (2 since / so far) I was in high school. That means I've watched every movie she's made (3 for / since) 1993, except for *Vicky Cristina Barcelona*. I (4 yet / still) haven't seen that one, but I plan to see it soon. I've (5 still / always) loved Penélope's work. I've (6 since / always) been the first person in line at the theater when her movies open. Of the movies Penélope has made (7 lately / always), the most interesting ones to me are *To Rome with Love* and *I'm So Excited*. I think they're the (8 best / just) movies she's made (9 so far / still). I've (10 always / already) seen them twice!

B **PAIR WORK** Take turns asking and answering the questions. Use the present perfect in all your answers.

1 Is there a movie you've always wanted to see?
2 Have you seen any good movies recently?
3 What's the best movie you've ever seen?
4 What's the worst movie you've ever seen?
5 How many movies have you seen so far this month?
6 Is there a classic movie that you still haven't seen?

DIGITAL
MORE
EXERCISES

DIGITAL
FLASH
CARDS
VOCABULARY *Explanations for being late*

A ▶1:19 Read and listen. Then listen again and repeat.

I overslept.

I missed the bus.

I couldn't get a taxi.

I couldn't find a parking space.

I got stuck in traffic.

B **PAIR WORK** Think of two other explanations for being late.

C ►1:20 **LISTEN TO ACTIVATE VOCABULARY** Listen to the conversations. Complete the sentences, inferring the information and using the Vocabulary.

1 Ted's late because he ....

2 Maude probably ....

3 They're going to be late because they ....

4 First they .... Then they probably ....

PRONUNCIATION *Reduction of* h

►1:21 Notice how the sound /h/ often disappears in natural speech. Read and listen. Then listen again and repeat.

1 How long have you waited?

2 Where have you been?

3 What has he read about the film?

4 When did he buy the tickets?

5 What's her favorite movie?

6 Who's his favorite star?

CONVERSATION MODEL

A ►1:22 Read and listen to someone apologize for being late.

A: Have you been here long?

B: For about ten minutes.

A: Sorry I'm late. I got stuck in traffic. Did you get tickets?

B: Yes. But the 8:00 show for *The Love Boat* is sold out. I got tickets for *Paradise Island.* I hope that's OK.

A: That's fine. How much do I owe?

B: Nothing. It's on me.

A: Well, thanks! Next time it's my treat.

B ►1:23 **RHYTHM AND INTONATION** Listen again and repeat. Then practice the Conversation Model with a partner.

NOW YOU CAN Apologize for being late

A Add four more movies to the showtimes.

B **CONVERSATION ACTIVATOR** With a partner, personalize the Conversation Model with your movies and explanations. Then change roles.

A: Have you been here long?

B: For ....

A: Sorry I'm late. I .... Did you get tickets?

B: Yes. But .... I hope that's OK.

A: ....

Stuck in Traffic	7:00	9:00	11:00
	7:30	9:35	[7:30 sold out]
	7:45	10:20	midnight
	8:00	11:00	[8:00 sold out]
	7:50	10:10	

DON'T STOP!

• Say more about the movie.
• Offer to pay.
• Discuss what to do after the show.

RECYCLE THIS LANGUAGE.

[Titanic 3] is sold out.
We missed __.
It started __ minutes ago.
I've already seen __.
That's past my bedtime!
I'm not a [Naomi Watts] fan.

I've heard [it's spectacular].
They say [it's pretty violent].
How much do I owe?
It's on me.
It's my treat.

C **CHANGE PARTNERS** Practice the conversation again, making other changes.

GOAL Discuss preferences for movie genres

VOCABULARY *Movie genres*

A ▶1:24 Read and listen. Then listen again and repeat.

an action film

a horror film

a science-fiction film

an animated film

a comedy

a drama

a documentary

a musical

B **PAIR WORK** Compare your favorite movies for each genre.

❝ My favorite animated film is *Frozen*. ❞

C ▶1:25 **LISTEN TO INFER** Listen and write the genre for each movie in the chart. Then circle the movie if the people decided to see it.

D **DISCUSSION** Which movies sound good to you? Listen again if necessary. Explain your choices.

Movie	Genre
1 *The Bottom of the Sea*	
2 *Tango in Tap Shoes*	
3 *The Ant Who Wouldn't Die*	
4 *Chickens Never Wear Shoes*	
5 *Goldilocks Grows Up*	
6 *The Equalizer*	
7 *Twelve Angry Women*	
8 *City Under the Sea*	

GRAMMAR *Ways to express wants and preferences*

Would like

Use <u>would like</u> + an infinitive (<u>to</u> + a base form) to politely express or ask about wants.

I'd **like** to go to the movies.
Would she **like** to see *The Dancer*?
What would your friends **like** to do?

I She We They	**'d like**	**to see** a comedy.

Would rather

Use <u>would rather</u> + a base form to express or ask about a preference between two or more activities.

Would your children **rather see** an animated film or an action film?
What **would** you **rather do**: go to a movie or a play?
She'**d rather see** a less violent film than *Gangs of New York*.

Use <u>would rather not</u> + a base form to express a negative preference.

We'**d rather not watch** TV tonight.

I He We They	**'d rather**	**see** a drama.

Yes / no questions

Would you **like** to see a documentary?
Would they **rather** stay home?

short answers

Yes, I would. / No, I wouldn't.
Yes, they would. / No, they wouldn't.
OR No, they'd rather not.

Be careful!
Would you rather see *Titanic*? Yes, **I would.**
    NOT Yes, I ~~would rather~~.
Would they like to go out tonight? Yes, **they would.**
    NOT Yes, they ~~would like~~.
Would your parents like to go to the early show?
    Yes, **they would.** NOT Yes, ~~they'd~~.

GRAMMAR BOOSTER p. 128
• Expressing preferences: review, expansion, and common errors.

A GRAMMAR PRACTICE Complete the conversations about wants and preferences.

1 A: (I like / I'd like) to see *Star Wars X* again. Would you? It's at the CineMax.

   B: Actually, (I'd rather. / I'd rather not.) Let's stay home.

2 A: (Do you like / Would you like) to stream something on TV?

   B: Yes, (I'd like. / I would.)

3 A: What would you rather (see / to see): a science fiction film or a comedy?

   B: Me? (I'd rather / I rather) see a science fiction movie.

4 A: There's a musical and a horror movie on TV. (Would / Does) your husband rather see the horror movie?

   B: Yes, (he would rather. / he would.)

5 A: My sister (would like to / would like) go to the movies on Friday.

   B: Great. (I would / I would like), too.

B PAIR WORK Use <u>would like</u> and <u>would rather</u> to ask your partner about movies he or she would like to see and his or her preferences.

> ❝ Would you like to see *Boomerang*? ❞

> ❝ What would you rather see: a documentary or a drama? ❞

CONVERSATION MODEL

A ▶1:26 Read and listen to people discussing their movie preferences.

A: What would you rather do: stay home and stream a movie or go to the theater?

B: I'd rather go out. Is that OK?

A: Sure! . . . Would you rather see *Horror City* or *Love in Paris*?

B: Are you kidding? I can't stand horror movies, and to tell you the truth, I'm not that big on love stories.

A: Well, how about a documentary? *The Great Wall of China* is playing, too. I've heard it's great.

B: That works for me!

▶1:28 **Ways to agree on a plan**
That works for me.
It's a deal!
Great idea!

B ▶1:27 **RHYTHM AND INTONATION** Listen again and repeat. Then practice the Conversation Model with a partner.

NOW YOU CAN Discuss preferences for movie genres

A CONVERSATION ACTIVATOR Write the names of some movies. With a partner, change the Conversation Model, using your own movies. Then change roles.

A: What would you rather do: stay home and stream a movie or go to the theater?
B: I'd rather .... Is that OK?
A: .... Would you rather see .... or .... ?
B: Are you kidding? I can't stand .... , and to tell you the truth, I ....
A: Well, how about .... ?

DON'T STOP!
• Say more about the movies and express more movie preferences.

B CHANGE PARTNERS Change the conversation again, using different movies.

RECYCLE THIS LANGUAGE.

I don't like / hate / love __s. Have you ever seen __? I missed it. Frankly, __ .	I'm not that big on __s. I've heard / They say it's [fascinating, thrilling, frightening, disgusting].

GOAL Describe and recommend movies

BEFORE YOU LISTEN

A ▶1:29 **VOCABULARY • *Adjectives to describe movies*** Read and listen. Then listen again and repeat.

funny something that makes you laugh

hilarious very, very funny

silly not serious; almost stupid

boring not interesting

weird very strange or unusual, in a negative way

unforgettable something you are going to remember

romantic about love

thought-provoking something that makes you think

violent bloody; with a lot of fighting and killing

B **PAIR WORK** Write the title of a movie for each adjective. Then tell your partner about your choices.

a funny movie	
a hilarious movie	
a silly movie	
a boring movie	
a weird movie	
an unforgettable movie	
a romantic movie	
a thought-provoking movie	
a violent movie	

LISTENING COMPREHENSION

A ▶1:30 **LISTEN FOR MAIN IDEAS** Listen to the movie reviewer. Write a check next to the movies he recommends, and write an **X** next to the ones he doesn't.

1 ☐ *Popcorn*   2 ☐ *The Vacation*   3 ☐ *Aquamundo*   4 ☐ *Wolf Babies*

B ▶1:31 **LISTEN TO INFER** Listen carefully to each movie review again. Based on the reviewer's opinion, circle one or more adjectives to describe each movie.

1 *Popcorn* (weird / funny / boring)   3 *Aquamundo* (boring / violent / thought-provoking)

2 *The Vacation* (romantic / violent / unforgettable)   4 *Wolf Babies* (violent / boring / hilarious)

C ▶1:32 **LISTENING: DICTATION** Listen to the following excerpts from the reviews. Complete each statement, based on what you hear.

POPCORN ★

① First up is *Popcorn*, a new .... starring David Bodine and Judy Crabbe. ② Unfortunately, *Popcorn* is a complete waste of ....

THE VACATION ★ ★ ★ ★ ★

③ Our next film, *The Vacation*, is a well-acted and .... ④ I highly .... wonderful ....

AQUAMUNDO ★ ★ ★

⑤ *Aquamundo* is no .... film; it's based on real scientific research. ⑥ A .... film. Don't ....

WOLF BABIES ★ ★ ★

⑦ Adults will find the story .... , but children won't forget these .... , scary scenes for a long time.

A **PAIR WORK** Read the short movie reviews and choose the movie you think sounds the most interesting. Then compare movie choices. Explain your reasons.

WHAT'S YOUR ALL-TIME FAVORITE MOVIE?

Phil Ito Toronto, CANADA

I've just seen *Tootsie*. What a great movie—perhaps one of the most hilarious romantic comedies of all time. Before I saw the movie, I thought the plot sounded both weird and silly, but it wasn't. Dustin Hoffman stars as out-of-work actor Michael Dorsey, who dresses as a woman to get a part on a TV drama. But problems begin when he falls in love with his co-star, Jessica Lange, who doesn't know Michael is a man. If you want a good laugh, be sure to see this funny, funny film!

Angela Teixeira Fortaleza, BRAZIL

When someone says that documentaries are boring, I say, "You have to see *Grizzly Man*," one of the most thought-provoking documentaries of all time. This 2005 movie by German director Werner Herzog tells the true story of the life and death of Timothy Treadwell, who lived for 13 years among bears in the Alaska wilderness. Treadwell believed that he could live near bears without danger. In the end, however, Treadwell and his girlfriend are killed by bears. Even if you would rather avoid violence, go to see *Grizzly Man* because there is no actual violence on screen.

Rebecca Lane Miami, USA

I've just seen *Casablanca* for the hundredth time. It's the most romantic movie in the world, and there's no movie I would rather see. Humphrey Bogart and Ingrid Bergman star as former lovers who meet after many years. They're still in love and have to make some difficult choices. The ending is unforgettable and always makes me cry. This movie was made in 1942, but it's always "new." I guess that's what makes it a classic.

B **NOTEPADDING** Write notes about a movie you've seen recently. (It's OK if you don't have all the information.)

Title of film:

Genre:

Stars:

Director or producer:

Adjectives that describe the movie:

What the movie is about:

C **GROUP WORK** Describe and recommend the movies on your notepads. Use adjectives from the Vocabulary and other adjectives you know.

DON'T STOP!

• Ask questions.

↻ RECYCLE THIS LANGUAGE.

Questions	More adjectives	
Was it [funny / silly / scary]?	thrilling	exciting
Who was in it?	fascinating	great
What kind of movie was it?	frightening	interesting
Do you recommend it?	disgusting	bloody
What was it about?	scary	unusual
	popular	terrific
	awful	pretty good

Text-mining (optional)
Look at the reviews in Exercise A. Find and underline three words or phrases that were new to you. Use them in your Group Work. For example: "falls in love with . . ."

BEFORE YOU READ

WARM-UP At what age do you think it's safe to permit children to see violent movies and TV shows? Explain.

READING ▶1:33

Can Violent Movies or TV Programs Harm Children?

Many people say that children have become more aggressive in recent years—that is, they are more likely to fight with their friends, sisters, and brothers. A number of scientific studies have reported that watching violence can, in fact, cause a growth in aggression. According to the research, two kinds of programs and movies encourage aggressive behavior in young children more than others: (1) realistic violent action programs and movies, and (2) violent cartoons.

One disturbing conclusion is that the effects of violent viewing last for many years. One study showed that children who watched violent TV programs when they were 8 years old were more likely to behave aggressively at age 18. Furthermore, as adults they were more likely to be convicted of violent crimes, such as child abuse and murder.

Studies have also demonstrated that watching violent movies and TV shows can affect children's attitudes towards violence in the world around them. Children who watch a lot of fighting and bloodshed tend to find it "normal" and may accept more violence in society. They may even begin to commit violent acts themselves.

Very often, characters in movies and on television who commit violent crimes are not sorry for their actions and don't face consequences or punishment. When children see fictional characters who are criminals like these, they learn that doing bad things is OK. For children, who are growing and developing, this is a bad message. It's important for them to see that our society doesn't tolerate crime.

So what can we do? With young children, we have the power to control the TV programs and movies they watch, so we can protect them from seeing any violence at all. However, with older children it's impossible to completely prevent their exposure to violence. But we can try to limit the number of hours they spend watching it. And when children have seen a violent film or TV show, it's important to discuss it with them, to help them understand that violence is not a normal part of life.

A **UNDERSTAND FROM CONTEXT** Circle the correct word or phrase to complete each statement, according to the information in the article.

1 (A realistic / An aggressive) person is someone who is likely to fight with others.

2 Scientific studies have reported that some kinds of movies and TV programs can (limit / encourage) aggressive behavior.

3 One kind of violent crime is (murder / bad behavior).

4 A word that means almost the same thing as hurt is (help / harm).

5 It's difficult to (permit / prevent) older children from seeing any violence on TV and in movies.

6 Research has suggested that (a consequence / an advantage) of watching violent films is aggressive behavior.

B **CONFIRM CONTENT** Discuss the questions, using the information in the article. Then share your answers with the class.

1 According to the article, what are some ways that viewing violence can affect children?

2 What kinds of programs and movies are most harmful?

3 According to the article, some studies show that viewing violence can have effects that last for many years. What are some of these long-term effects?

4 What bad "message" can come from violent programs and movies?

5 What suggestions does the article make to help parents prevent the bad effects of violent TV programs and movies in very young children? In older children?

C **EVALUATE IDEAS** Do you agree with the article that "violence is not a normal part of life"? Explain your answer.

DIGITAL MORE RCISES

NOW YOU CAN Discuss effects of violence on viewers

A Complete the chart with three films or television shows you know. Rate the level of violence from 0 to 3, with 3 being the most violent.

Title	Medium	Level of Violence
The Dark Knight Rises	film	2

0 = not violent, 1 = somewhat violent, 2 = violent, 3 = ultra violent

B **NOTEPADDING** Write notes about the most violent film or TV show on your chart.

Should children see it? Why? / Why not?

Is it OK for adults to see it? Why? / Why not?

C **DISCUSSION** Discuss the effects of violence on viewers. Use the information from your notepad to help you express your ideas. Here are some questions to consider in your discussion:

* In your opinion, are there some people who should not see violent movies? If so, who?

* Is the effect of viewing violence the same in children and adults?

* Does violence encourage adults to behave aggressively?

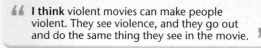

❝ **I think** violent movies can make people violent. They see violence, and they go out and do the same thing they see in the movie. ❞

❝ **I agree** . . . ❞

❝ **I disagree. I feel that** . . . ❞

Text-mining (optional)
Find and underline three words or phrases in the Reading that were new to you. Use them in your Discussion.
For example: "a bad message."

REVIEW

A ▶1:34 Listen to the conversation about movies. Check the correct description of each movie.

1
- ☐ a romantic film
- ☐ a documentary about Brazil
- ☐ a horror movie

2
- ☐ an animated police story
- ☐ a weird love story
- ☐ an unforgettable comedy

3
- ☐ an unforgettable movie
- ☐ a weird police story
- ☐ an animated children's film

4
- ☐ a documentary about cooking ham
- ☐ a musical tragedy
- ☐ a silly comedy

5
- ☐ a documentary
- ☐ a movie only for adults
- ☐ an animated musical

6
- ☐ a comedy
- ☐ an animated film
- ☐ a drama

B Complete the conversations. Choose the correct verbs and adverbial expressions, and write the movie genres.

1 A: (Have you seen / Did you see) a good .... (just / lately)?
   B: To tell you the truth, no. But last night (we've seen / we saw) a great ....

2 A: How many times (have they seen / did they see) *War of the Worlds*?
   B: That remake of the old .... movie? I think (they saw it / they've seen it) twice (still / so far).

3 A: Sally is such a .... fan. How long (has she waited / did she wait) for this film to come out on DVD?
   B: She's waited (for / since) at least six months.

4 A: I (didn't see / haven't seen) a .... as good as *Twelve Angry Men*.
   B: Really? I (lately / still) (didn't see / haven't seen) it.

C Complete each statement or question with <u>for</u> or <u>since</u>.

1 That film has played at the Metroplex .... two weeks.
2 *The Talking Parrot* has been available to stream online .... last Tuesday.
3 I've loved animated movies .... I was a child.
4 Have you been here .... more than an hour?
5 I've been a fan of science fiction movies .... over thirty years.
6 I've been in the ticket line .... 6:30!

For additional language practice...

🎵 TOP NOTCH POP • Lyrics p. 153
"Better Late Than Never"

WRITING

Write two paragraphs about violence in movies and on TV. Explain why some people think it's harmful and why others think it isn't.

WRITING BOOSTER p. 144
- Paragraphs
- Topic sentences
- Guidance for this writing exercise

ORAL REVIEW

PAIR WORK

1 With a partner, guess the genre of the three movies. Imagine what the movies are about and choose actors to star in the movies. Present your ideas to the class. Use the following as a model.

We think "Love in Paradise" is a romantic movie. It's about a man and a woman who meet and fall in love in Hawaii.

2 Create a conversation for one of the couples. Say as much as you can. For example:

It's 7:30. Did we miss "Love in Paradise"?

SOLD OUT

Cult of Blood
7:20 9:00 Midnight

Love in Paradise
7:15 9:45

Ticket to the Moon
8:00 10:00

NOW I CAN

☐ Apologize for being late.
☐ Discuss preferences for movie genres.
☐ Describe and recommend movies.
☐ Discuss effects of violence on viewers.

COMMUNICATION GOALS
1 Leave and take a message.
2 Check into a hotel.
3 Request housekeeping services.
4 Choose a hotel.

PREVIEW

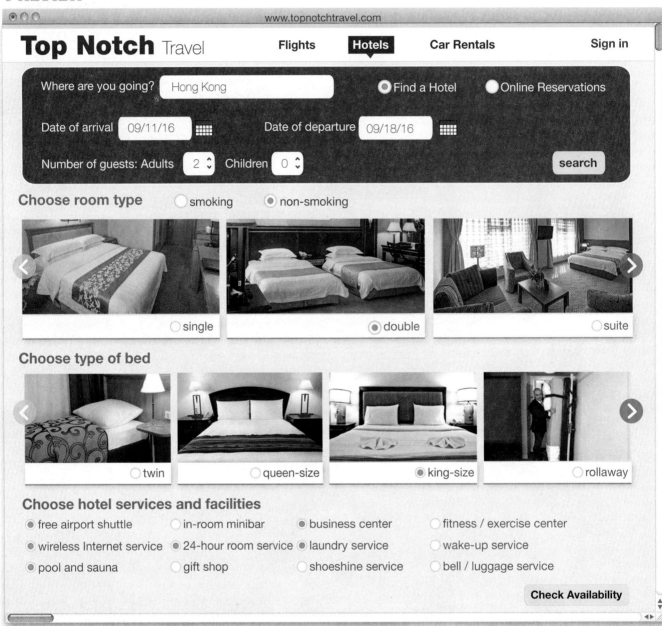

www.topnotchtravel.com

Top Notch Travel   Flights   **Hotels**   Car Rentals   Sign in

Where are you going? Hong Kong   ●Find a Hotel   ○Online Reservations

Date of arrival 09/11/16   Date of departure 09/18/16

Number of guests: Adults 2   Children 0   search

Choose room type   ○smoking   ●non-smoking

○single   ●double   ○suite

Choose type of bed

○twin   ○queen-size   ●king-size   ○rollaway

Choose hotel services and facilities

● free airport shuttle   ○ in-room minibar   ● business center   ○ fitness / exercise center
● wireless Internet service   ● 24-hour room service   ● laundry service   ○ wake-up service
● pool and sauna   ○ gift shop   ○ shoeshine service   ○ bell / luggage service

Check Availability

DIGITAL FLASH CARDS

A ▶2:02 **VOCABULARY** • *Hotel room types and kinds of beds* Read and listen. Then listen again and repeat.

1 a single room	**4** a smoking room	**7** a queen-size bed
2 a double room	**5** a non-smoking room	**8** a king-size bed
3 a suite	**6** a twin bed	**9** a rollaway bed

B **PAIR WORK** Have you—or has someone you know—ever stayed at a hotel? Tell your partner about it, using the Vocabulary and the facilities from the website.

ENGLISH FOR TODAY'S WORLD
Understand English speakers from
different language backgrounds.
Guest = Korean speaker

C ▶ 2:03 **PHOTO STORY** Read and listen to someone checking out of a hotel.

Guest: Good morning. I'm checking out of Room 604.

Clerk: I'll be happy to help you with that. Was your stay satisfactory?

Guest: Yes. Very nice. Thanks.

Clerk: Did you have anything from the minibar last night?

Guest: Just a bottle of water.

Clerk: OK. Let me add that to your bill.

Clerk: And would you like to put this on your Vista card?

Guest: Yes, I would, please. By the way, I need to go to the airport.

Clerk: Certainly. If you're in a hurry, I'll call you a taxi. But if you'd rather take the free airport shuttle, there's one leaving in twenty minutes.

Guest: Great. I'll take the shuttle. Why pay for a taxi? And that'll give me time to pick up a few things at the gift shop before I leave.

Clerk: No problem. I'll ask the bellman to give you a hand with your luggage. He'll let you know when the shuttle's here.

Guest: Thanks so much.

Clerk: You're welcome. Have a safe trip, and we hope to see you again.

D **FOCUS ON LANGUAGE** Find underlined words and phrases in the Photo Story with the same meaning.

1 pay with   2 help   3 leaving   4 OK   5 don't have much time

E **THINK AND EXPLAIN** Explain why each statement is false, using information from the Photo Story.

1 The guest is staying for a few more days.   3 The guest pays the bill in cash.
2 The guest has complaints about the hotel.   4 The shuttle is arriving in an hour.

SPEAKING

Match each picture with a hotel service from the list. Which services are important to you? Explain why.

1 ....   2 ....   3 ....   4 ....

5 ....   6 ....   7 ....

▶ 2:04 **Hotel services**
airport shuttle
bell service
laundry service
minibar
room service
shoeshine service
wake-up service

❝ Wake-up service is important to me. When I travel for business, we usually have very early meetings. ❞

GOAL Leave and take a message

CONVERSATION MODEL

A ▶2:05 Read and listen to someone leaving a message.

A: Hello? I'd like to speak to Anne Smith. She's a guest.

B: I'll ring that room for you . . . I'm sorry. She's not answering. Would you like to leave a message?

A: Yes. Please tell her Tim Klein called. I'll meet her at the hotel at three this afternoon.

B: Is that all?

A: Yes, thanks.

B ▶2:06 **RHYTHM AND INTONATION** Listen again and repeat. Then practice the Conversation Model with a partner.

GRAMMAR *The future with* <u>will</u>

You can use <u>will</u> **or** <u>won't</u> **+ a base form to talk about the future.**

Affirmative statements

He **will call** back tomorrow.

Negative statements

We **won't be** at the hotel this afternoon.

Questions

Will she **meet** us at the restaurant?   Yes, she will. / No, she won't.
Will they **take** a taxi to the hotel?   Yes, they will. / No, they won't.

When **will** the shuttle **arrive**? (In about ten minutes.)
What **will** you **do** in New York? (Visit the Empire State Building.)
Where **will** they **go** on their next vacation? (Probably Los Angeles.)

Who **will** Ana **call** when she arrives? (She'll call the front desk.)
BUT
Who **will call** the front desk? (Ana will.)

> **Contractions**
> will = 'll
> will not = **won't**

> **Remember:** You can also talk about the future with <u>be going to</u>, the present continuous, or the simple present tense.
> I'm **going to call** again at 4:00.
> They're **meeting** at noon at the hotel.
> She **arrives** on PanAir Flight 24 tonight.

> **GRAMMAR BOOSTER** p. 129
> • Will: expansion
>   <u>Will</u> and <u>be going to</u>
>   other uses of <u>will</u>
> • Can, should, and have to: future meaning

A **FIND THE GRAMMAR** Look at the Conversation Model again. Circle two uses of <u>will</u>.

B **GRAMMAR PRACTICE** Complete the statements and questions in the messages, using <u>will</u> or <u>won't</u>. Use contractions when possible.

1 Message for Ms. Yalmaz: Ms. Calloway called. .... back later this evening.
   she / call

2 Message for Mr. Ballinger: .... at the Clayton Hotel until after 5:00.
   your colleagues / not / be

3 Message for John Torrence: Your boss called. .... a recommendation for a
   he / need
   nice restaurant for tonight.

4 Message from Mark Smith: .... us to the airport after the meeting?
   who / take

5 Message for Ms. Harris: .... at the airport before 6:00.
   your brother / not / arrive

6 Message from Janis Torres: .... at 3:00 tomorrow, London time.
   the conference call / start

7 Message from Mrs. Park: .... come in to the office early tomorrow?
   I / have to

8 Message for Ms. Grady: .... us tomorrow?
   where / you / meet

DIGITAL
MORE
EXERCISES

C ▶ 2:07 **LISTEN FOR DETAILS** Listen to the phone messages. Then listen again and complete each message slip, according to the information you hear. Use the future with <u>will</u> in each message.

1

☎ **PHONE MESSAGE**

FOR: _Judy Diller_

FROM: ☑ Mr. ☐ Ms.
        ☐ Mrs. ☐ Miss _Pearl_

☐ Please call   ☐ Will call again
☐ Wants to see you   ☐ Returned your call

Message: _He'll be . . ._
_____
_____

2

☎ **PHONE MESSAGE**

FOR: _Hank Pitt_

FROM: ☐ Mr. ☐ Ms.
        ☐ Mrs. ☐ Miss _____

☐ Please call   ☐ Will call again
☐ Wants to see you   ☐ Returned your call

Message: _____
_____

3

☎ **PHONE MESSAGE**

FOR: _Collin Mack_

FROM: ☐ Mr. ☐ Ms.
        ☐ Mrs. ☐ Miss _____

☐ Please call   ☐ Will call again
☐ Wants to see you   ☐ Returned your call

Message: _____
_____

4

☎ **PHONE MESSAGE**

FOR: _Patricia Carlton_

FROM: ☐ Mr. ☐ Ms.
        ☐ Mrs. ☐ Miss _____

☐ Please call   ☐ Will call again
☐ Wants to see you   ☐ Returned your call

Message: _____
_____

PRONUNCIATION *Contractions with* <u>will</u>

A ▶ 2:08 Notice that each contraction is one syllable. Read and listen. Then listen again and repeat.

1 I'll call back later.

2 She'll be at the Frank Hotel.

3 He'll bring his laptop to the meeting.

4 We'll need a taxi.

5 You'll have to leave at 6:30.

6 They'll meet you in twenty minutes.

B Look at the message slips you wrote in Exercise C above. Read each message aloud, using the correct pronunciation of the contracted form of <u>will</u>.

NOW YOU CAN Leave and take a message

A **FRAME YOUR IDEAS** On a separate sheet of paper, write four messages you could leave someone.

B **CONVERSATION ACTIVATOR** With a partner, change the Conversation Model. Leave your own messages. Your partner completes the message slip. Then change roles.

A: Hello? I'd like to speak to ....

B: I'll ring that room for you . . . I'm sorry. ....
Would you like to leave a message?

A: Yes. Please tell ....

B: Is that all?

A: ....

WHILE YOU WERE OUT . . .

FOR: _____

☐ Mr. ☐ Ms. ☐ Mrs. ☐ Miss _____ called.

Phone: _____

☐ Please call back
☐ Will call again

Message: _____
_____

DON'T STOP!

• Leave another message.
• Confirm that you've understood the message correctly.
• Ask for more information.

🔄 **RECYCLE THIS LANGUAGE.**

How do you spell your last name?
Could you please spell that for me?
Could you please repeat that?
What's your __?

C **CHANGE PARTNERS** Leave other messages.

GOAL Check into a hotel

GRAMMAR *The real conditional*

Conditional sentences express the results of actions or conditions.

if clause (the condition)   **result clause (the result)**
If the business center is still open,   I'll check my e-mail.

Real conditional sentences express factual or future results. When the result is future, use <u>will</u> in the result clause.
(A factual result: Use present tense in both clauses.)
If a hotel room **has** wireless Internet, guests **don't have to go** to a business center to check e-mail.
(A future result: Use present tense in the <u>if</u> clause and future with <u>will</u> in the result clause.)
If she **checks in** early, she**'ll get** the room she wants.

Questions
If they **don't have** a non-smoking room, **will** you **stay** at a different hotel?
Where **will** you **go** if they **don't have** a room for tonight?
If there **are** no rental cars at the airport, what **will** they **do**?

Be careful!
Never use <u>will</u> in the <u>if</u> clause.
If you hurry, you'll catch the shuttle.   NOT   If you ~~will hurry~~, you'll catch the shuttle.

In conditional sentences, the clauses can be reversed with no change in meaning.
In writing, use a comma when the <u>if</u> clause comes first.
If the fitness center is still open, I'll go swimming.
I'll go swimming if the fitness center is still open.

> **GRAMMAR BOOSTER** p. 130
> • The real conditional: present and future; usage and common errors

A **UNDERSTAND THE GRAMMAR** Write <u>factual</u> if the conditional sentence expresses a fact. Write <u>future</u> if it expresses a future result.

.... **1** If you make your reservation in advance, you save a lot of money.

.... **2** She'll miss the 11:00 shuttle if she doesn't check out early today.

.... **3** If a guest is in a hurry, a taxi is faster than the shuttle.

.... **4** We will call your room this evening if there are any messages.

.... **5** If you request a suite, you usually get free breakfasts.

.... **6** You'll have to pay a daily fee if you want wireless service.

B **GRAMMAR PRACTICE** Complete the real conditional statements and questions with correct forms of the verbs.

1 .... to order breakfast at the restaurant if ....
     you / not / be able   you / not / hurry

2 If .... a suite on their next cruise, ... a lot more comfortable.
       they / get   they / be

3 .... a room with a king-size bed if .... affordable?
     you / reserve   it / be

4 .... me a hand if .... help with my luggage?
    someone / give   I / need

5 Who .... if .... laundry service?
        we / call   we / need

6 .... pay if .... wireless Internet service?
     I / have to   I / use

7 If .... a rollaway bed, ... it to your room.
     you / request   someone / bring

8 Where .... if .... to make copies?
       she / go   she / need

DIGITAL
MORE
EXERCISES

CONVERSATION MODEL

A ▶2:09 Read and listen to someone checking into a hotel.

A: Hi. I'm checking in. The name's Baker.
B: Let's see. That's a double for two nights. Non-smoking?
A: That's right.
B: May I have your credit card?
A: Here you go. By the way, is the restaurant still open?
B: It closes at 9:00. But if you hurry, you'll make it.
A: Thanks.

B ▶2:10 **RHYTHM AND INTONATION** Listen again and repeat. Then practice the Conversation Model with a partner.

C ▶2:11 **LISTEN FOR DETAILS** Listen to guests check into a hotel. Complete the information about what each guest needs.

	Type of bed(s)	Non-smoking room?	Bell service?
1		☐	☐
2		☐	☐
3		☐	☐
4		☐	☐

NOW YOU CAN Check into a hotel

A **CONVERSATION ACTIVATOR** With a partner, role-play checking into a hotel. Change the room and bed type, and ask about a hotel facility from the pictures. Then change roles.

A: Hi, I'm checking in. The name's ....
B: Let's see. That's a .... for .... night(s). Non-smoking?
A: ....
B: May I have your credit card?
A: Here you go. By the way, is the .... still open?
B: It closes at .... But if you hurry, you'll make it.
A: ....

DON'T STOP!
- Ask about other services and facilities.

Business Center Hours
9 AM to 5 PM

Fitness Center Hours
6 AM to 9 PM

Sauna Hours
11 AM to 8 PM

Pool Hours
6 AM to 10 PM

Gift Shop Hours
8 AM to 9 PM

B **CHANGE PARTNERS** Practice the conversation again. Discuss other room and bed types and hotel facilities.

BEFORE YOU LISTEN

DIGITAL FLASH CARDS

A ▶2:12 **VOCABULARY • *Hotel room amenities and services*** Read and listen. Then listen again and repeat.

We need. . .

extra towels.

extra hangers.

skirt hangers.

an iron.

a hair dryer.

Could someone. . .

make up
the room?

turn down
the beds?

pick up the
laundry?

bring up a
newspaper?

take away
the dishes?

B **EXPAND THE VOCABULARY** Complete the statements and questions with other items you know. Then compare items with a partner.

1 We need extra ....*glasses and coffee cups*........................... .

2 We also need ....

3 Could someone pick up my .... ?

4 Could someone bring up .... ?

5 Could someone take away the .... ?

Ideas
- dirty towels
- breakfast / lunch / dinner
- bags / luggage
- a coffee maker
- a rollaway bed
- laundry bags
- (your own idea) ___

LISTENING COMPREHENSION

A ▶2:13 **LISTEN FOR MAIN IDEAS** Decide if the guests are satisfied or not. Then explain your answers.

Room 586
☐ Satisfied
☐ Not satisfied

Room 587
☐ Satisfied
☐ Not satisfied

B ▶2:14 **LISTEN FOR DETAILS** Listen again and complete each statement.

Room 586
The guest wants someone to take away .... , bring up .... and .... , and pick up ....

Room 587
The guest wants someone to .... the .... , bring up .... , and .... the ....

A **PAIR WORK** Look at the pictures. With a partner, discuss what you think each hotel guest is saying.

B **PAIR WORK** Role-play a telephone conversation between one of the guests and hotel staff.
Use your ideas from Exercise A. Then change roles. Start like this:

A: Hello. Room Service. How can I help you?
B: Hi, I'd like to order . . .

DON'T STOP!
• Complain about other problems.
• Ask about the hotel facilities and services.
• Leave a message for another hotel guest.

🔄 **RECYCLE THIS LANGUAGE.**

Hotel staff	Hotel guest
Hello, [Gift Shop].	Is the [sauna] still open?
Is everything OK?	What time does the [business center] close / open?
I'm sorry to hear that.	
Let me check.	Could someone __?
Certainly.	The __ isn't / aren't working.
I'll be happy to help you with that.	The __ won't turn on.
	I need __.
	I'd like to order [room service].
	I'd like to leave a message for __.

BEFORE YOU READ

EXPLORE YOUR IDEAS What do you think is the best way to get information about a hotel?

☐ by word of mouth
☐ from an online hotel booking service
☐ from a travel guide book
☐ from a travel agency
☐ other ....

READING ▶ 2:15

www.topnotchtravel.com

Top Notch Travel   Flights   **Hotels**   Car Rentals   Sign in

Our best picks for New York City   ● $ Budget   ● $$ Moderately priced   ● $$$ Expensive   ● $$$$ Very expensive

The Plaza Hotel $$$$ Most famous

Located just across from New York's fabulous Central Park, this is as near as it gets to the best shopping along New York's famous Fifth Avenue. This 1907 hotel, with its beautiful fountain, is a famous location in many popular movies and books. Rub shoulders with the rich and famous. Attentive hotel staff available on every floor—service doesn't get much better than this!
Amenities: 4 restaurants • full-service spa and health club • concierge • business center • 24-hour room service • twice-daily housekeeping service

The Plaza Hotel's famous fountain

More Info

Broadway at Times Square Hotel $$ Most convenient

In a great location—next to Times Square and the best Broadway musicals and plays, this convenient hotel is two blocks from the subway, ten minutes from Rockefeller Center, and ten blocks from the Museum of Modern Art.
Amenities: 24-hour business center • 24-hour front desk • fitness center • free Wi-Fi • wake-up service

Rockefeller Center

More Info

YOTEL $$$ Most high-tech

Popular with young travelers, this very cool high-tech hotel, located only two blocks from the Port Authority bus station, offers automatic electronic check-in and robot bell service! A kitchen on every floor offers free hot drinks and a way to prepare your own food. And super-strong Wi-Fi service makes connecting to the Internet fast and headache-free. Enjoy Yotel's Latin-Asian restaurant and entertainment, or hang out at New York's largest roof garden.
Amenities: 24-hour front desk • laundry • currency exchange • tour desk • ATM • concierge service • fitness center • free Wi-Fi

The Manhattan Skyline

More Info

Casablanca Hotel $$ Most unusual

Conveniently located near Times Square and more than fifty restaurants and two major museums, this award-winning hotel has lots of atmosphere—it's decorated in a colorful authentic Moroccan style. Its friendly, helpful staff make your stay an experience you won't forget, and it's also surprisingly affordable!
Amenities: 24-hour front desk • free Wi-Fi • free passes to nearby health club • free breakfast • free coffee, tea, cookies, and fruit all day • Italian restaurant on first floor

Times Square

More Info

For the budget minded

Hotel Pennsylvania $
A huge 1,700-room hotel and a great value. Traveling with your cat or dog? Pets are welcome.
The Hotel Newton $
Even though it's far from many of New York's most popular attractions, it features large clean rooms and wonderfully comfortable beds for a good night's sleep. Sorry, no pets.
The Gershwin Hotel $
Around the corner from the Empire State Building, this artistic 1903 historic hotel is just a short walk to Grand Central Station and the United Nations Building. Every room displays a famous artist's painting.

Grand Central Station

More Info

A DRAW CONCLUSIONS Complete each statement with the name of a hotel (or hotels) from the Reading. Then compare choices and reasons with a partner.

1 On his vacations, Carl Ryan, 43, likes to stay near the Theater District. If he stays at
the Broadway at Times Square Hotel or the Casablanca Hotel , he'll be near the Theater District.

2 Stella Korman, 35, doesn't like the beds in most hotels. However, if she stays at
.... , her room will definitely have a great bed.

3 Mark and Nancy Birdsall (22 and 21) are always online. If they stay at the
.... , the Wi-Fi service is not only free, but it's really fast.

4 Lucy Lee, 36, will pay more for a hotel that is very comfortable and offers a lot of services. If she stays at
.... , she'll be very happy.

5 Brenda Rey prefers hotels that are different and interesting. If she stays at
.... , she'll find them different from other hotels.

6 James Kay always travels with his dog, Louie. If he stays at .... , Louie will have to stay home.

DIGITAL
MORE
RCISES

B IDENTIFY SUPPORTING DETAILS Compare responses in Exercise A with a partner. If you disagree, explain why you chose a particular hotel.

NOW YOU CAN Choose a hotel

A FRAME YOUR IDEAS What's important to you in choosing a hotel? Rate the following factors on a scale of 1 to 5.

not important ⟷ very important

price	1	– 2	– 3	– 4	– 5
room size	1	– 2	– 3	– 4	– 5
cleanliness	1	– 2	– 3	– 4	– 5
location	1	– 2	– 3	– 4	– 5
service	1	– 2	– 3	– 4	– 5
amenities	1	– 2	– 3	– 4	– 5
atmosphere	1	– 2	– 3	– 4	– 5

B PAIR WORK Find each hotel from the Reading on the map. Discuss the advantages and disadvantages of each. Then choose a hotel.

> 66 The Casablanca Hotel sounds like it has a lot of atmosphere. It's affordable, and the location is good. 99

Text-mining (optional)
Find three words or phrases in the Reading that were new to you. Use them in your Pair Work.
For example: "conveniently located."

C SURVEY AND DISCUSSION Take a survey of how many classmates chose each hotel. Discuss and explain your choices.

> 66 Most of us chose the Hotel Newton because . . . 99

A ▶2:16 Listen to the phone conversations in a hotel. Then listen again and complete each statement, using words from the box.

| bell | room | dinner | hangers | make up the room |
| laundry | shoeshine | towels | wake-up | turn down the beds |

1 She wants someone to bring up .... She also needs .... service.

2 He needs .... service, and he wants someone to bring up extra ....

3 She wants someone to .... , and she wants someone to bring up extra ....

4 He needs .... service and .... service.

B What hotel room or bed type should each guest ask for?

1 Ms. Gleason is traveling alone. She doesn't need much space. ....*a single room*....

2 Mr. and Mrs. Vanite and their twelve-year-old son Boris are checking into a room with one king-size bed. ....

3 Mike Krause plans to use his room for business meetings with important customers. ....

4 George Nack is a big man, and he's very tall. He needs a good night's sleep for an important meeting tomorrow. ....

5 Paul Krohn's company wants him to save some money by sharing a room with a colleague. ....

C Write real conditional statements and questions. Use the correct forms of the verbs and correct punctuation.

1 if / it / rain this morning / Mona / not go / to the beach
If it rains this morning, Mona won't go to the beach...............

2 if / you / walk to the restaurant / you / be there in fifteen minutes
....

3 Mr. Wang / get a better job / if / he / do well on the English test tomorrow
....

4 what / Karl / do / if / the airline / cancels his flight
.... ?

5 if / you / not like / your room / who / you / call
.... ?

For additional language practice . . .

♫ TOP NOTCH **POP** • Lyrics p. 153
"Checking Out"

WRITING

Write a paragraph about the hotel you chose in Lesson 4. Explain why you would like to stay there. What are its advantages and disadvantages?

I would like to stay at the Hotel Casablanca.
Atmosphere is very important to me and . . .

WRITING BOOSTER p. 145
• Avoiding sentence fragments with because or since
• Guidance for this writing exercise

ORAL REVIEW

PAIR WORK

1 Create a conversation between the hotel guest in Room 816 and the woman at the front desk. Ask for hotel services or complain about a problem. Start like this:

Hello? Is this the front desk?

2 Create a conversation between the man at the front desk and the caller. Use <u>will</u>. Complete the message slip. Start like this:

A: *Front desk. Can I help you?*
B: *Yes, thanks. I'd like to leave a message for . . .*

3 Create a conversation between the two men at the front desk. Check into or check out of the hotel. Discuss hotel amenities, services, and schedules. Start like this:

Hi. I'm checking in. The name's ....

☎ **PHONE MESSAGE**

FOR: _____
FROM: ☐ Mr.   ☐ Ms.
       ☐ Mrs.   ☐ Miss _____
☐ Please call   ☐ Will call again
☐ Wants to see you   ☐ Returned your call

Message: _____
_____
_____

THE BELMAR

DIRECTORY

Business Center	2
9:00 AM – 4:00 PM	
Gift Shop	Lobby
9:00 AM – 9:00 PM	
Fitness Center	3
6:00 AM – 10:00 PM	
Spa	5
10:00 AM – 3:00 PM	
Belmar Café	12
8:00 AM – 11:00 PM	

✓ **NOW I CAN**

☐ Leave and take a message.
☐ Check into a hotel.
☐ Request housekeeping services.
☐ Choose a hotel.

 **UNIT 4 Cars and Driving**

PREVIEW

COMMUNICATION GOALS

1 Discuss a car accident.
2 Describe a car problem.
3 Rent a car.
4 Discuss good and bad driving.

Eight Habits of Bad Drivers
How many drivers in your city . . .

❶ speed?
☐none ☐some ☐most ☐all

❷ tailgate?
☐none ☐some ☐most ☐all

❸ talk on the phone?
☐none ☐some ☐most ☐all

❹ text while driving?
☐none ☐some ☐most ☐all

❺ weave through traffic?
☐none ☐some ☐most ☐all

❻ don't stop at red lights?
☐none ☐some ☐most ☐all

❼ don't signal when turning?
☐none ☐some ☐most ☐all

❽ pass in a no-passing zone?
☐none ☐some ☐most ☐all

 A ▶2:19 **VOCABULARY • Bad driving habits** Read and listen. Then listen again and repeat.

> speed
> tailgate
> talk on the phone
> text while driving
> weave through traffic
> not stop at red lights
> not signal when turning
> pass in a no-passing zone

B PAIR WORK Compare surveys with a partner. Discuss and explain your answers.

❝ Some drivers in my city talk on the phone while they're driving. It's terrible. ❞

❝ Lots of taxi drivers turn without signaling. I don't like that. ❞

C ▶2:20 **PHOTO STORY** Read and listen to a conversation between two old friends.

15 minutes later

Mason: Brad! Long time no see.

Brad: Mason! You're right. It *has* been a long time. How've you been?

Mason: I can't complain. What about you? How's the family?

Brad: Great! I was just going in here to pick up a present for Marissa. Tomorrow's our fifth anniversary.

Mason: Congratulations! . . . Hey! Let's have a cup of coffee and catch up on old times. There's a nice coffee place right around the corner.

Brad: You won't believe what I just saw.

Mason: What?

Brad: This taxi was coming around the corner, and he hit a bus! Someone said the guy was texting while he was driving.

Mason: You've got to be kidding! Was anyone hurt?

Brad: I don't think so.

Mason: Thank goodness for that.

Brad: I just can't stop thinking about that accident.

Mason: I know. The driving in this city has always been bad, but now everyone's texting and talking on the phone instead of paying attention to the road.

Brad: You can say that again! You shouldn't multitask while you're driving a car.

D **FOCUS ON LANGUAGE** Match each numbered sentence with one of the quotations from the Photo Story.

1 I've been fine.

2 I totally agree with you.

3 I'm so happy for you!

4 I'm glad nothing terrible happened.

5 Really? That's unbelievable.

6 It's great to see you again.

a "Congratulations!"

b "I can't complain."

c "Long time no see."

d "Thank goodness for that."

e "You can say that again!"

f "You've got to be kidding!"

E **THINK AND EXPLAIN** Discuss with a partner.

1 What did Mason mean when he said, "Let's have a cup of coffee and catch up on old times."?

2 What did Brad mean when he said, "You shouldn't multitask while you're driving a car"?

SPEAKING

DISCUSSION Discuss an accident you know about. Answer the questions.

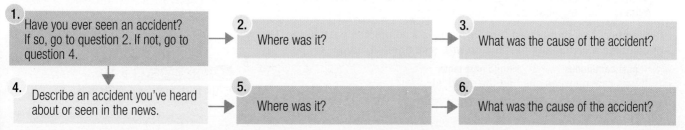

1. Have you ever seen an accident? If so, go to question 2. If not, go to question 4.

2. Where was it?

3. What was the cause of the accident?

4. Describe an accident you've heard about or seen in the news.

5. Where was it?

6. What was the cause of the accident?

GOAL Discuss a car accident

VOCABULARY *Car parts*

A ▶ 2:21 Read and listen. Then listen again and repeat.

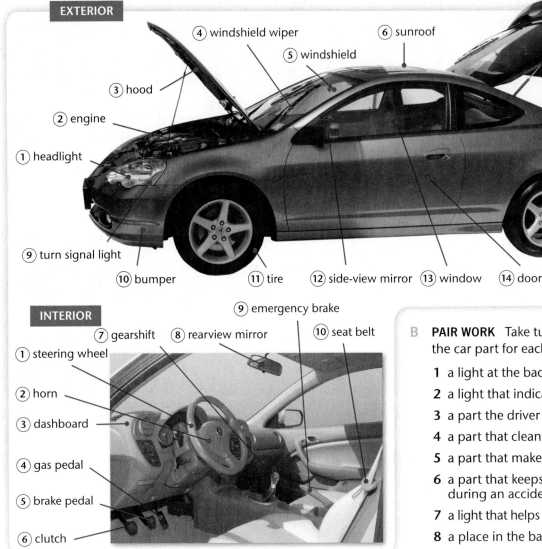

EXTERIOR

④ windshield wiper
⑥ sunroof
⑤ windshield
③ hood
⑦ trunk
② engine
⑧ taillight
① headlight
⑨ turn signal light
⑩ bumper ⑪ tire ⑫ side-view mirror ⑬ window ⑭ door

INTERIOR

⑨ emergency brake
⑦ gearshift ⑧ rearview mirror ⑩ seat belt
① steering wheel
② horn
③ dashboard
④ gas pedal
⑤ brake pedal
⑥ clutch

B **PAIR WORK** Take turns identifying the car part for each definition.

1 a light at the back of the car
2 a light that indicates a turn
3 a part the driver uses to turn the car
4 a part that cleans the front window
5 a part that makes the car go faster
6 a part that keeps passengers safe during an accident
7 a light that helps the driver see the road
8 a place in the back for carrying things

GRAMMAR *The past continuous*

The past continuous describes an activity that continued during a period of time in the past or at a specific time in the past.

The car **was making** a funny sound while they **were driving**.
Were the headlights **working**? (Yes, they were. / No, they weren't.)
Who **was driving** your car at 10:00 last night?

Remember: The simple past tense describes a <u>completed</u> past action. Use <u>when</u> to combine a continuing past action with a completed action.

   past continuous   simple past tense
It **was raining** when she **had** the accident.

Form the past continuous with <u>was</u> or <u>were</u> and a present participle.
The other driver **was speeding**.

GRAMMAR BOOSTER p. 131
• The past continuous: other uses

A GRAMMAR PRACTICE Complete the paragraph with the past continuous and the simple past tense.

I .... an accident yesterday. I .... slowly and I'm
       1 have   2 drive
sure I .... attention. But I .... for a phone call. When
       3 pay   4 wait
the phone ...., I .... it. Suddenly, the car in front of me
                5 ring   6 answer
................................, and I .... it. I certainly ....
      7 stop   8 hit   9 learn
my lesson! Luckily, I .... when I .... the accident.
            10 not speed   11 have

B ▶ 2:22 LISTEN TO ACTIVATE VOCABULARY Listen to the conversations about accidents.
Write the number of each conversation in the box under the picture. Then listen again
and write the car part or parts that were damaged in each accident.

☐ ....   ☐ ....   ☐ ....   ☐ ....

CONVERSATION MODEL

A ▶ 2:23 Read and listen to a conversation about a
car accident.

A: I had an accident.

B: I'm so sorry. Are you OK?

A: I'm fine. No one was hurt.

B: Thank goodness. How did it happen?

A: Well, the other driver was tailgating,
and he hit my car.

B: Oh, no! Was there much damage?

A: No. I'll only have to replace a taillight.

▶ 2:25 Ways to respond

With concern	With relief
I'm so sorry.	Thank goodness.
Oh, no!	What a relief!
How awful!	That's good.
I'm sorry to hear that.	
That's terrible.	

B ▶ 2:24 RHYTHM AND INTONATION Listen again and repeat.
Then practice the Conversation Model with a partner.

NOW YOU CAN Discuss a car accident

A Write what the driver was doing. Use the past continuous.

B CONVERSATION ACTIVATOR With a partner, change the
Conversation Model, using the pictures. Then change roles.

A: I had an accident.
B: .... Are you OK?
A: ....
B: .... How did it happen?
A: Well, ... , and .... hit my car.
B: .... Was there much damage?
A: ....

DON'T STOP!

• Ask more questions
about location, other
damage, the other
driver, etc.

The driver wasn't
paying attention.

....

....

....

C CHANGE PARTNERS Discuss other accidents.

GOAL Describe a car problem

DIGITAL FLASH CARDS

VOCABULARY *Phrasal verbs for talking about cars*

A ▶2:26 Read and listen. Then listen again and repeat.

| turn on | turn off | pick up | fill up | drop off |

B Complete the sentences with the two parts of each phrasal verb.

1 The car's almost out of gas. Let's go in here so I can .... it ....

2 It's raining, and I can't .... the windshield wipers .... They aren't working.

3 Can I use your car this afternoon? I can .... it .... at 3:30 if you don't need it then.

4 We have to return the rental car before 6:00. Let's .... it .... early at the airport and get something to eat, OK?

5 I can't .... the air conditioning .... It's freezing in here!

GRAMMAR *Placement of direct objects with phrasal verbs*

> **Phrasal verbs contain a verb and a particle that together have their own meaning.**
>
> main verb   particle
> turn   +   on   =   start (a machine)
>
> **Many phrasal verbs are separable. This means that a direct object noun can come before or after the particle. <u>Turn on</u>, <u>turn off</u>, <u>pick up</u>, <u>drop off</u>, and <u>fill up</u> are separable.**
>
>   direct object   direct object
> I'll **drop off** the car. OR I'll **drop** the car **off**.
>
> **Be careful! With a separable phrasal verb, if the direct object is a pronoun, it must come before the particle.**
>
> I'll **drop** it **off**. (NOT I'll ~~drop off it~~.)
> Did you **fill** them **up**? (NOT Did you ~~fill up them~~?)
> Where will they **pick** us **up**? (NOT Where will they ~~pick up us~~?)

> GRAMMAR BOOSTER p. 131
> • Nouns and pronouns: review

DIGITAL VIDEO COACH

PRONUNCIATION *Stress of particles in phrasal verbs*

A ▶2:27 Stress changes when an object pronoun comes before the particle. Read and listen. Then listen again and repeat.

1 A: I'd like to pick up my car.
   B: OK. What time can you pick it up?

2 A: They need to drop off the keys.
   B: Great. When do they want to drop them off?

B GRAMMAR / VOCABULARY PRACTICE Write statements or questions, placing the direct objects correctly. Then practice reading the sentences aloud with a partner. Use correct stress.

1 The taillights aren't working. (can't / I / on / them / turn) ....

2 They're expecting the car at 10:00. (off / drop / 10:00 / at / I'll / it) ....

3 It's too cold for air conditioning. (button / which / off / it / turns) .... ?

4 Thanks for fixing the car. (it / pick / what time / I / can / up) .... ?

5 The car is almost out of gas. (up / please / fill / it) ....

CONVERSATION MODEL

A ▶2:28 Read and listen to someone describing a car problem.

A: I'm dropping off my car.

B: Was everything OK?

A: Well, actually, the windshield wipers aren't working.

B: I'm sorry to hear that. Any other problems?

A: No. That's it.

B: Is the gas tank full?

A: Yes. I just filled it up.

B ▶2:29 **RHYTHM AND INTONATION** Listen again and repeat. Then practice the Conversation Model with a partner.

C FIND THE GRAMMAR Find and underline two direct objects in the Conversation Model.

NOW YOU CAN Describe a car problem

A NOTEPADDING Write two or more possible car parts for each car problem.

won't open / close:	*the sunroof, the hood . . .*
won't turn on / off:	
(is / are) making a funny sound:	
(isn't / aren't) working:	

B CONVERSATION ACTIVATOR With a partner, change the Conversation Model. Report a problem with a car. Use your notepad for ideas. Then change roles and problems.

A: I'm dropping off my car.
B: Was everything OK?
A: Well, actually ....
B: .... Any other problems?
A: ....

C CHANGE PARTNERS Describe other car problems.

D OPTION Role-play a conversation in which you report an accident when you drop off a rental car. Describe the accident. Say what you were doing when you had the accident, using the past continuous. Then change roles. Start like this:

A: I'm dropping off my car. I had an accident . . .

RECYCLE THIS LANGUAGE.

Oh, no!	Yes, the [taillight]
How did it happen?	is broken.
Is there any damage?	isn't working.
Was anyone hurt?	won't turn on / off.
	is making a funny sound.

LESSON **3** | **GOAL** Rent a car

BEFORE YOU LISTEN

DIGITAL
FLASH
CARDS

A ▶2:30 **VOCABULARY • *Car types*** Read and listen. Then listen again and repeat.

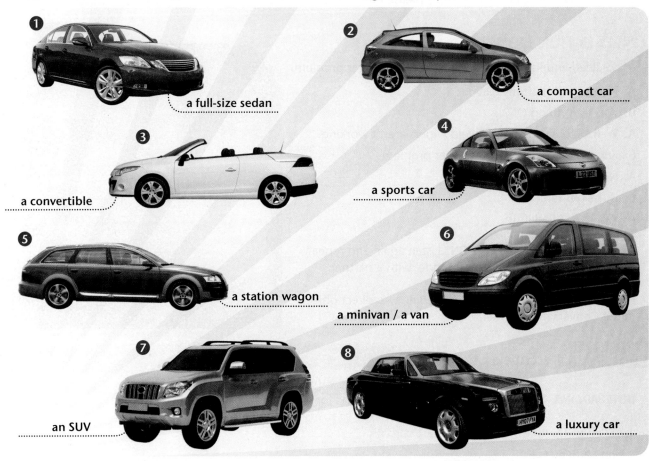

❶ a full-size sedan
❷ a compact car
❸ a convertible
❹ a sports car
❺ a station wagon
❻ a minivan / a van
❼ an SUV
❽ a luxury car

B **PAIR WORK** Which car would you like to drive? Which car would you *not* like to drive? Discuss with a partner, using the Vocabulary.

❝ I'd like to drive the luxury car because people will think I have a lot of money. ❞

❝ Really? I'd rather drive the convertible. It's really cool. ❞

LISTENING COMPREHENSION

A ▶2:31 **LISTEN FOR DETAILS** Listen. Write the car type that the speakers discuss in each conversation.

1 .... 2 .... 3 .... 4 ....

B ▶2:32 **LISTEN TO SUMMARIZE** Listen again. Write a check mark if the caller rented a car. Then listen again. Write the reasons the other callers <u>didn't</u> rent a car.

☐ 1 ....

☐ 2 ....

☐ 3 ....

☐ 4 ....

A **PAIR WORK** Read about each customer at Wheels Around the World, an international car rental company. Choose the best type of car for each person. Discuss reasons with your partner.

> " A compact car is good for driving in a big city. It is easier to park in a small parking space. "

1

Background: Ms. Potter is a businesswoman from Boston, in the U.S. She is flying to Dallas to attend a business meeting. She doesn't have a lot of luggage. She only needs a car for local travel around Dallas.

Customer Profile

Car type: ....
Reason: ....

4

Background: Mr. Lucena is a banker from Curitiba, Brazil. His son is getting married in Valparaíso, Chile. He wants to drive to Valparaíso from the airport in Santiago, Chile with his wife and their two other children for the wedding. They have a lot of clothes and presents for the wedding.

Customer Profile

Car type: ....
Reason: ....

2

Background: Ms. Park is a tourist from Busan, Korea, visiting western Australia with her cousin. They enjoy hiking and fishing, and they're planning a road trip through the Lake District. They plan to drive on some rough roads, so they want a car with four-wheel drive.

Customer Profile

Car type: ....
Reason: ....

5

Background: Dr. Andrade is from Pereira, Colombia. He's flying to an international medical conference in La Paz, Bolivia. He has invited three doctors to dinner and after-dinner entertainment. He likes to drive.

Customer Profile

Car type: ....
Reason: ....

3

Background: Ms. Kimura is a tourist from Osaka, Japan, visiting national parks and cities in the western part of the U.S. with her husband and their three children. They plan to do a lot of shopping, too.

Customer Profile

Car type: ....
Reason: ....

B **NOTEPADDING** Plan a trip for which <u>you</u> need a rental car.

Destination	Pickup date	Drop off date	Number of companions	Activities

C **ROLE PLAY** With a partner, role-play a phone call to Wheels Around the World to rent a car for the trip you planned on your notepad. Choose one of the car types from the Vocabulary on page 44. Discuss the trip and your needs. Then change roles.

 RECYCLE THIS LANGUAGE.

Agent
Hello. Wheels Around the World.
What kind of car [do you need / would you like]?
How many people are you traveling with?
When will you [pick up / drop off] the car?
Where will you drop off the car?
Would you rather rent [a full-sized sedan] or [an SUV]?

Caller
I'd like to make a reservation.
I'd like a [compact car].
I'd rather have a [van].
I'm traveling with [my husband].
It's a [business trip / vacation].
I [have / don't have] a lot of luggage.
Do you accept credit cards?

BEFORE YOU READ

A ▶2:33 **VOCABULARY** • *Driving behavior* Read and listen. Then listen again and repeat.

DIGITAL FLASH CARDS

Bad or aggressive drivers . . .

honk their horns

stare at other drivers

gesture at other drivers

flash their lights at other drivers

Good drivers . . .

pay attention

observe the speed limit

maintain a safe following distance

And don't forget . . .
speed
tailgate
talk on the phone
text while driving
weave through traffic
not stop at stoplights
not signal while turning
pass in a no-passing zone

B **WARM-UP** In your opinion, which of the bad and aggressive driving habits are the most dangerous? Why?

READING ▶2:34

FEATURE ARTICLE

Six Tips for Defensive Driving

We all know that not everyone drives well. Some people tailgate, gesture, weave through traffic, and honk—classic signs of the aggressive driving that causes one third of all car crashes. But more and more people are now talking on the phone, eating, and even watching TV as they drive—examples of the multitasking and inattentive driving that is a growing cause of accidents. Although we can't control the actions of other drivers, the following defensive driving tips can help us reduce the risks caused by our own driving and the bad driving of others.

1 **Slow down.** Driving too fast for weather or road conditions gives you less time to react to dangers on the road ahead of you. Also, as you increase your speed, your car becomes harder to control and takes longer to come to a stop.

2 **Follow the "3-second rule."** The greatest chance of a collision is in front of you. Maintaining a safe following distance of three seconds behind the car in front of you will give you enough time to react if that car slows or stops suddenly.

3 **Pay attention to your surroundings.** Be aware of where other vehicles are and what is happening on the road. Check your rearview and side-view mirrors frequently. Before changing lanes, always look over your shoulder to check your "blind spots"—areas to the side and rear of your car that aren't visible in your mirrors.

4 **Signal your intentions early.** Use turn signals to let other drivers know what you're going to do before you do it. This helps other drivers understand your plans so they can make their own defensive driving decisions.

5 **Expect the unexpected.** Assume that other drivers will make mistakes. Plan ahead what you will do if another driver breaks a traffic law or cuts you off. For example, don't assume that a vehicle coming to a stop sign or a red light is going to stop. Be prepared to stop your own car if necessary.

6 **Don't take others' aggressive driving personally.** Other people will drive badly. They're not thinking about you. If you permit them to make you angry, it can affect your own driving and lead to an accident. When other drivers show signs of aggressive driving, just slow down or pull over to let them pass.

A UNDERSTAND FROM CONTEXT Circle the correct word or phrase to complete each statement.

1 A person who is doing more than one activity at the same time is (multitasking / driving defensively).

2 Following the "3-second rule" means maintaining a safe (road condition / following distance).

3 Tailgating, gesturing, and honking are three examples of (inattentive / aggressive) driving.

4 Not paying attention is an example of (inattentive / aggressive) driving.

5 *Collision* and *crash* are two words that mean (danger / accident).

6 A part of the road that you can't see in your mirrors is called a (blind spot / lane).

DIGITAL
MORE
RCISES

B CRITICAL THINKING How can defensive driving help drivers avoid accidents? Explain your opinion, using the Vocabulary and examples from the Reading or from your own experience.

NOW YOU CAN Discuss good and bad driving

A PAIR WORK Complete the survey and then compare surveys with a partner.

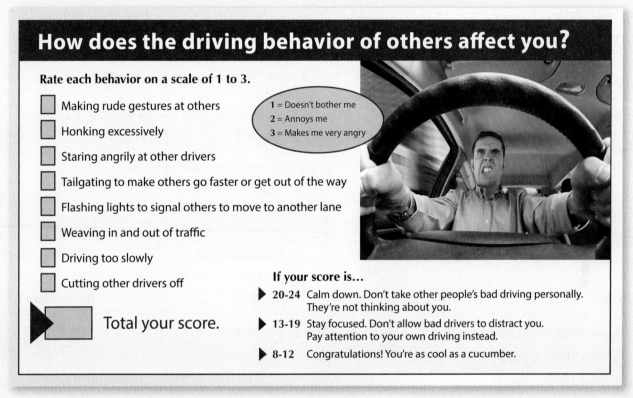

How does the driving behavior of others affect you?

Rate each behavior on a scale of 1 to 3.

☐ Making rude gestures at others

☐ Honking excessively

☐ Staring angrily at other drivers

☐ Tailgating to make others go faster or get out of the way

☐ Flashing lights to signal others to move to another lane

☐ Weaving in and out of traffic

☐ Driving too slowly

☐ Cutting other drivers off

1 = Doesn't bother me
2 = Annoys me
3 = Makes me very angry

☐ Total your score.

If your score is...

▶ 20-24 Calm down. Don't take other people's bad driving personally. They're not thinking about you.

▶ 13-19 Stay focused. Don't allow bad drivers to distract you. Pay attention to your own driving instead.

▶ 8-12 Congratulations! You're as cool as a cucumber.

B NOTEPADDING Describe what good and bad drivers do. Use the Vocabulary.

Good drivers . . .	Aggressive drivers . . .
use their turn signals	flash their lights at others

C DISCUSSION Discuss good and bad driving. What percentage of drivers do you think are bad or aggressive? Use your notepad for support.

Text-mining (optional)
Find and underline three words or phrases in the Reading that were new to you. Use them in your Discussion.
  For example: "slow down."

A ▶2:35 Listen to the conversations. Then complete the statements with words and phrases for bad or aggressive driving.

1 The other driver just .... them ....

2 Jim's mother says he's ....

3 The driver behind them is .... at them.

4 The driver opened his window and .... at them.

5 The driver is .... because he wants to pass.

6 The driver is ....

7 The driver is .... at them.

B Read each definition. Write the name of the car part.

1 a window on the top of the car:
   ....

2 a part that stops the car: ....

3 a window the driver looks through to see the cars in front: ....

4 a place where the driver can find information about speed and amount of gas: ....

5 a part that people wear to avoid injuries in an accident: ....

6 a part that prevents the car from moving when it's parked: ....

C Complete each statement or question about driving. Use the past continuous or the simple past tense.

1 I .... , and I .... an accident.
        not pay attention   have

2 The other driver .... at the stop sign, and she .... a seat belt.
        not stop   not wear

3 He .... on a cell phone, and his car .... my trunk.
       talk   damage

4 Who .... when the accident ....?
       drive   occur

5 Where .... they .... when they .... the accident?
        stand   see

D Complete each conversation, putting the phrasal verbs and objects in order.

1 A: Won't the car start?
   B: No. I can't ....
        it / turn / on

2 A: Do you need gas?
   B: Yes. Please ....
        up / fill / it

3 A: Hey, you haven't turned on your headlights.
   B: Oops. Thanks. I can't believe I forgot
   to ....
       turn / on / them

4 A: Can All Star Limo drive us to the airport?
   B: Yes. They'll .... at 5:30.
        us / pick / up

For additional language practice . . .

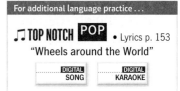

♫ TOP NOTCH POP • Lyrics p. 153
"Wheels around the World"

DIGITAL SONG   DIGITAL KARAOKE

WRITING

Write a short paragraph about the differences between good and bad drivers. Include language from pages 38, 44, and 46 in your paragraph.

WRITING BOOSTER p. 146
• Connecting words and sentences: And, In addition, Furthermore, and Therefore
• Guidance for this writing exercise

ORAL REVIEW

GROUP STORY Together, create a story about the pictures. Each person adds one sentence to the story. Begin with January 16. Use the past continuous and the simple past tense in your story. Start like this:

They picked up their rental car in Temuco on January 16 . . .

PAIR WORK

1 Create conversations for the people in the first three pictures. For example:

   A: *We'd like to rent a car.*
   B: *Certainly. What kind of a car do you need?*

2 Create a phone conversation for the fourth picture. The woman reports the accident to Multi Car Rentals. The agent responds. Say as much as you can. For example:

   We had an accident. My husband was . . .

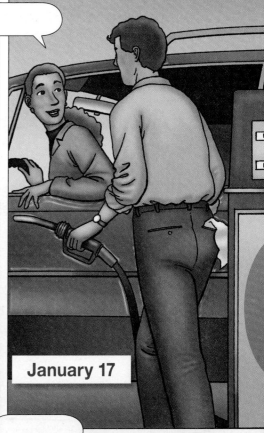

January 16

MULTI CAR RENTALS
Temuco, Chile

Pucon, Chile

JANUARY 16
ARRIVAL
14:45

January 17

January 18

80

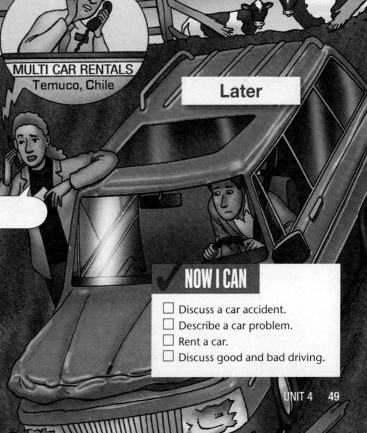

MULTI CAR RENTALS
Temuco, Chile

Later

✓ NOW I CAN

☐ Discuss a car accident.
☐ Describe a car problem.
☐ Rent a car.
☐ Discuss good and bad driving.

UNIT 5 Personal Care and Appearance

PREVIEW

THE APEX SPA and FITNESS CENTER

For a better-looking—and better—you!

WORLD CLASS TOP NOTCH SALON SERVICES ▾

haircuts

facials

shaves

FULLY EQUIPPED SPA ▾

manicures

pedicures

massage:
Swedish, therapeutic, or shiatsu

GROUP EXERCISE CLASSES ▾

yoga . . .

kickboxing . . .

STATE OF THE ART GYM ▾

Pilates . . .

spinning . . . and more

The latest in exercise equipment

Make an appointment with our personal trainers.

A ▶3:02 **VOCABULARY** • *Salon services* Read and listen. Then listen again and repeat.

| a haircut | a facial | a shave | a manicure | a pedicure |

B **PAIR WORK** With a partner, discuss the Apex Club services. What are the advantages of combining exercise and fitness with spa and massage services in one club?

ENGLISH FOR TODAY'S WORLD
Understand English speakers from
different language backgrounds.
Receptionist = French speaker

C ▶3:03 **PHOTO STORY** Read and listen to a conversation in a spa salon.

Receptionist: Can I help you, sir?

Client: Would it be possible to get a massage? I don't have an appointment.

Receptionist: Well, actually, you're in luck. Our eleven o'clock just called to cancel his appointment.

Client: Terrific.

Receptionist: Let me show you to the dressing area.

Client: Thanks. Oh, while I'm at it, do you think I could get a haircut, too?

Receptionist: Yes. But you might have to wait a bit. We don't have anything until 12:00.

Client: Not a problem. By the way, how much will the massage and haircut come to?

Receptionist: Let's see . . . it will be 110 euros in all.

Client: Great. One more question. Is it customary to tip the staff?

Receptionist: Well, that's up to you. But most clients give the stylist and the masseuse a euro or two each.

D **FOCUS ON LANGUAGE** Answer the questions, using language from the Photo Story.

1 How does the client ask for a massage?

2 How does the receptionist indicate that the client can have a massage without an appointment?

3 How does the client ask about the price of a massage and a haircut?

4 What phrase does the receptionist use to tell the client the total cost of the salon services?

5 How does the client say "That's OK"?

6 What expression does the receptionist use to tell the client that the amount to tip is <u>his</u> decision?

SPEAKING

A **PERSONALIZE** Check the word or phrase that best describes how often you get these salon services. Then compare charts with a partner.

	weekly	monthly	once in a while	never	I do this for myself!
haircut	☐	☐	☐	☐	☐
facial	☐	☐	☐	☐	☐
shave	☐	☐	☐	☐	☐
manicure	☐	☐	☐	☐	☐
pedicure	☐	☐	☐	☐	☐
massage	☐	☐	☐	☐	☐

B **PAIR WORK** In your opinion, what is the value of each service? Compare opinions with a partner.

❝ I think massages are great for backaches. A massage helps me feel better. ❞

❝ A shave? Are you kidding? I do that myself. I don't go to salons! ❞

GOAL Ask for something in a store

DIGITAL
FLASH
CARDS

VOCABULARY *Personal care products*

A ▶3:04 Read and listen. Then listen again and repeat.

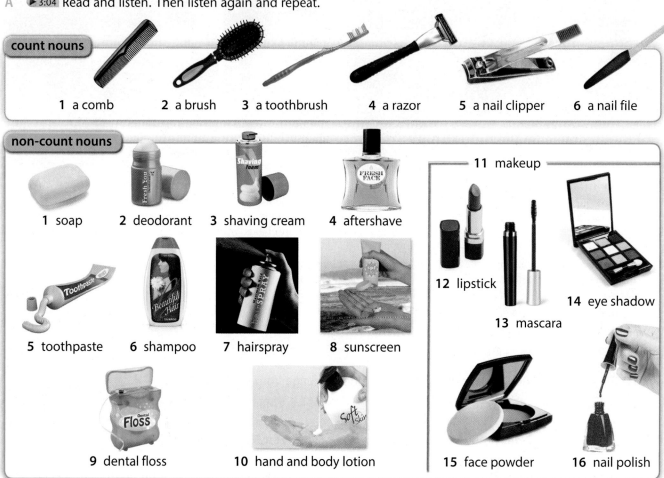

count nouns

1 a comb   2 a brush   3 a toothbrush   4 a razor   5 a nail clipper   6 a nail file

non-count nouns

1 soap   2 deodorant   3 shaving cream   4 aftershave

11 makeup

12 lipstick

13 mascara

14 eye shadow

5 toothpaste   6 shampoo   7 hairspray   8 sunscreen

9 dental floss   10 hand and body lotion

15 face powder   16 nail polish

B ▶3:05 **LISTEN TO INFER** Listen and circle the kind of product each ad describes.

1 Spring Rain (shampoo / deodorant)
2 Rose (soap / nail polish)
3 Pro-Tect (sunscreen / hand and body lotion)

4 All Over (face powder / hand and body lotion)
5 Scrubbie (toothpaste / shaving cream)
6 Maximum Hold (hairspray / shampoo)

GRAMMAR *Quantifiers for indefinite quantities and amounts*

Use <u>some</u> and <u>any</u> with both plural count nouns and non-count nouns.

<u>some</u>: **affirmative statements**

We bought some **combs**. Now we have some.
They need some soap. We have some.

<u>any</u>: **negative statements**

I don't have **any** razors. I don't want **any**.
We don't want **any** makeup. We don't need **any**.

<u>some</u> or <u>any</u>: **questions**

Do you want **any** aftershave?   OR   Do you want **some** aftershave?
Does she have **any** nail files?   OR   Does she have **some** nail files?

Use <u>a lot of</u> or <u>lots of</u> with both plural count nouns and non-count nouns in statements and questions. They have the same meaning.

That store has **a lot of** (or **lots of**) razors. They don't have **a lot of** (or **lots of**) sunscreen. Do they have **a lot of** (or **lots of**) makeup?

Use <u>many</u> and <u>much</u> in negative statements.

<u>many</u>: with plural count nouns   <u>much</u>: with non-count nouns

They don't have **many** brands of makeup.   The store doesn't have **much** toothpaste.

GRAMMAR BOOSTER p. 132
- <u>Some</u> and <u>any</u>: indefiniteness
- <u>Too many</u>, <u>too much</u>, and <u>enough</u>
- Comparative quantifiers <u>fewer</u> and <u>less</u>

GRAMMAR PRACTICE Complete the conversation between a husband and wife packing for a trip.

Dana: Do we have (1 any / many) shampoo?

Neil: Yes. We have (2 many / lots of) shampoo.

Dana: And Maggie uses (3 much / a lot of) sunscreen. Is there (4 many / any)?

Neil: No, there isn't (5 some / any). And we don't have (6 much / many) toothpaste, either.
          I can pick (7 some / any) up on my way back from work.

Dana: Hey, Adam's shaving now. Does he need (8 any / many) shaving cream?

Neil: He doesn't shave every day. He can use mine!

CONVERSATION MODEL

A   ▶3:06 Read and listen to someone looking for personal care products in a store.

   A: Excuse me. Where would I find sunscreen?

   B: Sunscreen? Have a look in the cosmetics section, in aisle 2.

   A: Actually, I did, and there wasn't any.

   B: I'm sorry. Let me get you some from the back. Anything else?

   A: Yes. I couldn't find any razors either.

   B: No problem. There are some over there. I'll show you.

B   ▶3:07 **RHYTHM AND INTONATION** Listen again and repeat.
Then practice the Conversation Model with a partner.

C   **FIND THE GRAMMAR** Find and underline the four quantifiers in the Conversation Model.

NOW YOU CAN Ask for something in a store

A   **CONVERSATION ACTIVATOR** With a partner, use the store directory to change the Conversation Model. Use the Vocabulary and quantifiers. Then change roles.

   A: Excuse me. Where would I find .... ?
   B: .... ? Have a look in ....
   A: Actually, I did, and there .... any.
   B: I'm sorry. Let me get you .... from the back. Anything else?
   A: ....

DON'T STOP!
- Ask about other personal care products.

🔄 **RECYCLE THIS LANGUAGE.**
How much [is that aftershave / are those nail clippers]?
Can I get this [shampoo] in a larger / smaller size?
Can I get this lipstick in [black]?
Do you have any cheaper [razors]?

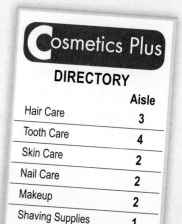

Cosmetics Plus

DIRECTORY

	Aisle
Hair Care	3
Tooth Care	4
Skin Care	2
Nail Care	2
Makeup	2
Shaving Supplies	1

B   **CHANGE PARTNERS** Practice the conversation again, asking for other products.

CONVERSATION MODEL

A ▶3:08 Read and listen to someone make an appointment for a haircut.

A: Hello. Classic Spa and Salon.

B: Hello. This is Monica Morgan. I'd like to make an appointment for a haircut.

A: When would you like to come in, Ms. Morgan?

B: Today, if possible.

A: Let me check. . . . Sean has an opening at 2:00.

B: Actually, that's a little early for me. Is someone available after 4:00?

A: Yes. Yelena can see you then.

B ▶3:09 **RHYTHM AND INTONATION** Listen again and repeat. Then practice the Conversation Model with a partner.

GRAMMAR *Indefinite pronouns: someone / no one / anyone*

Someone, no one, and anyone are indefinite pronouns. Each refers to an unnamed person. Use indefinite pronouns when the identity of the person is unknown or unimportant.

Affirmative statements

| Someone
No one | is available. |

| Someone
No one | is waiting for the manicurist. |

I saw **someone** at the front desk.

Questions

| Can | anyone
someone | wash my hair? |

| Is there | anyone
someone | at the front desk? |

| Did you see | anyone
someone | waiting for a shave? |

Negative statements

There isn't **anyone** waiting.
I didn't see **anyone** at the salon.

Be careful!

Use anyone, not no one, with the negative form of a verb.
I didn't speak to **anyone**.
NOT I didn't speak to ~~no one~~.

GRAMMAR BOOSTER p. 133
• Indefinite pronouns: something, anything, everything, and nothing

A ▶3:10 **LISTEN TO ACTIVATE VOCABULARY AND GRAMMAR** Listen to the conversations. Complete each statement with someone or anyone and the salon service(s).

1 They can't find .... to give her a .... this afternoon.

2 .... can give him a .... and a .... at 4:00.

3 There is .... who can give her a .... and a .... at 6:30.

4 There isn't .... who can give him a .... today.

B **GRAMMAR PRACTICE** Complete each statement or question with <u>someone</u>, <u>no one</u>, or <u>anyone</u>. In some cases, more than one answer is correct.

1 There's _someone (or no one)_ at the front desk.

2 They didn't tell .... it would be a long wait.

3 Did you see .... giving a manicure?

4 I didn't ask .... about the price.

5 There will be .... here to give you a pedicure in a few minutes.

6 .... can cut your hair at 12:30 if you can wait.

7 Please don't tell .... the price. It was very expensive!

8 .... called and left you this message while you were getting your shampoo.

9 There wasn't .... there when she called for an appointment.

10 I didn't speak to .... about the bad haircut.

11 .... told me the salon offers shiatsu massage now.

12 I don't have the nail file. I gave it to ....

DIGITAL
MORE
ERCISES

DIGITAL
VIDEO
COACH

PRONUNCIATION *Pronunciation of unstressed vowels*

A ▶ 3:11 The vowel in an unstressed syllable is often pronounced /ə/. Read and listen, paying attention to the syllable or syllables marked with /ə/. Then listen again and repeat.

1 ma ssage   2 fa cial   3 ma ni cure   4 pe di cure   5 de o do rant
    /ə/   /ə/   /ə/   /ə/   /ə/   /ə/

B Now practice saying the words on your own.

NOW YOU CAN **Make an appointment at a salon or spa**

DIGITAL
VIDEO

A **CONVERSATION ACTIVATOR** With a partner, change the Conversation Model, using services and staff from the list. Then change roles.

A: Hello. ....
B: Hello. This is .... I'd like to make an appointment for ....
A: When would you like to come in, ... ?
B: .... if possible.
A: Let me check. . . . . has an opening at ....
B: Actually, that's a little .... for me. Is someone available .... ?
A: Yes. .... can see you then.

DON'T STOP!
• Ask about other services.
• Ask about prices and payment.

🔁 **RECYCLE THIS LANGUAGE.**
Is someone available on / at __?
How much is [a pedicure]?
How long is [a massage]?
Can someone [wash my hair]?
I need [a shave].
Is the tip included?
Do you accept credit cards?

THE **APEX**
SPA and FITNESS CENTER

SERVICES	STAFF
haircut	Christopher/Diana
pedicure	Karin/Carlota
shave	Nick/Giorgio
manicure	Sonia/Marie
massage	Vladimir/Edouard
personal training	Igor/Betty

B **CHANGE PARTNERS** Practice the conversation again, making an appointment for other services.

BEFORE YOU READ

PREDICT Look at the photos and title of the article. What questions do you think the people will ask Dr. Weiss?

READING ▶ 3:12

Cosmetic surgery
. . . for everyone?

Contact Doctor Weiss at Personal Health Magazine: weiss@personalhealth.rx

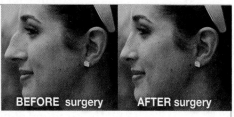

BEFORE surgery   AFTER surgery

Some people consider cosmetic surgery no more serious than visiting a spa or a salon. But others say, "I think I'll pass." They're aware that cosmetic surgery is, in fact, surgery, and surgery should never be taken lightly. Fitness editor Dr. Gail Weiss answers readers' questions about cosmetic surgery.

Dear Dr. Weiss:

I'm at my wits' end with my face. I have wrinkles and sun damage. I'm only 30, but I look 50. Do you think a face-lift is an option for me?

Josephine

Dear Josephine:

This popular and effective surgery lifts the face and the neck in one operation. But a face-lift is surgery, and afterwards you will have to stay home for a number of days. It takes time to recover. Before you decide to have a face-lift, ask your dermatologist or a cosmetic surgeon about a chemical peel. A chemical peel removes the top layer of skin and can improve the appearance of the skin without surgery. Compared to surgery, a half-hour visit to your dermatologist would be a piece of cake! Good luck!

Gail Weiss, M.D

Dear Dr. Weiss:

I'm a 24-year-old man who is already losing his hair. Dr. Weiss, I'm looking for a wife, and I'm afraid no woman will want to marry a 25-year-old bald guy. I need some advice.

Calvin

Dear Calvin:

There are several surgical procedures which a cosmetic surgeon can perform to help treat hair loss and restore hair for both men and women. But if that's not practical, remember that some of the world's most attractive men are bald!

Gail Weiss, M.D.

Dear Dr. Weiss:

When I was young, I was a chocoholic. I ate a lot of chocolate, but I never gained any weight. Now that I'm older, I can't eat anything without gaining weight! I've heard that liposuction is the answer to an overweight person's dreams. Is that true?

Dawson

Dear Dawson:

It's true that liposuction can remove fat deposits that don't respond to dieting and exercise, but it's expensive and can be dangerous. It would be a good idea to ask your doctor for some help in dieting first. Then, if you are unsuccessful, be sure to find a surgeon with a lot of experience before deciding on liposuction.

Gail Weiss, M.D.

A **PARAPHRASE** Find and circle each underlined expression in the article. Then circle the correct word or phrase to complete each statement.

1 If you say I think I'll pass, you mean ("No, thanks" / "That's a great idea").

2 If you are at your wits' end about something, you are (happy / unhappy) about it.

3 It takes time to recover means that you (will / won't) feel better immediately.

4 Something that is a piece of cake is (easy / difficult).

B **UNDERSTAND FROM CONTEXT** With a partner, find these procedures in the Reading and write a definition for each one.

1 liposuction ....

2 hair restoration ....

3 a face-lift ....

4 a chemical peel ....

C   **CONFIRM CONTENT AND APPLY INFORMATION**   Complete the chart with information from the article. Then, with a partner, give your own advice for each person.

	Problem	Dr. Weiss's advice	Your advice
Josephine			
Calvin			
Dawson			

NOW YOU CAN   Discuss ways to improve appearance

A   **FRAME YOUR IDEAS**   Take the opinion survey about ways to improve appearance.

How far would you go to improve your appearance?

Would you try ...	definitely	maybe	probably not	absolutely not!
diet?	○	○	○	○
exercise?	○	○	○	○
massage?	○	○	○	○
hair restoration?	○	○	○	○
cosmetics and makeup?	○	○	○	○
facials?	○	○	○	○
face-lifts?	○	○	○	○
liposuction?	○	○	○	○
chemical peels?	○	○	○	○

B   **NOTEPADDING**   Choose one method you would try and one method you would not try. On the notepad, write advantages and disadvantages.

Method	Advantage(s)	Disadvantage(s)
I would try diet.	free, safe	It's hard to do!

Method	Advantage(s)	Disadvantage(s)

C   **DISCUSSION**   What's the best way to improve your appearance? What ways would you NOT try? Explain. Use your notepad for support.

Text-mining (optional)
Find and underline three words or phrases in the Reading that were new to you. Use them in your Discussion.
For example: "surgical procedures."

GOAL Define the meaning of beauty

BEFORE YOU LISTEN

DIGITAL FLASH CARDS

A ▶3:13 **VOCABULARY** • *Discussing beauty* Read and listen. Then listen again and repeat.

physical features skin, hair, body shape and size, eyes, nose, mouth, etc.

beauty the physical features most people of a particular culture consider good-looking

attractive having a beautiful or pleasing physical or facial appearance

unattractive the opposite of *attractive*

youth appearing young; the opposite of looking old

health the general condition of one's body and how healthy one is

B **EXPLORE YOUR IDEAS** Write a statement or two describing, in your opinion, the characteristics of an attractive man or woman.

An attractive woman has long hair and dark eyes.

C **PAIR WORK** Use your statements to talk about the physical features you consider attractive for men and women. Use the Vocabulary.

❝ In my opinion, attractive people have . . . ❞

LISTENING COMPREHENSION

A ▶3:14 **LISTEN TO RECOGNIZE SOMEONE'S POINT OF VIEW** Listen to the interview. Check all of the statements that summarize Maya Prasad's and Ricardo Figueroa's ideas about beauty.

Maya Prasad

☐ I'm very lucky to be so beautiful.

☐ All the contestants were beautiful. I was just lucky.

☐ Physical beauty only lasts a short time.

☐ Love makes people beautiful.

Ricardo Figueroa

☐ Physical beauty is not important at all.

☐ Both physical beauty and inner beauty are important.

☐ Only inner beauty is important.

☐ Prasad represents an almost perfect combination of inner and outer beauty.

B ▶3:15 **LISTEN TO TAKE NOTES** Listen and take notes about what Figueroa says about each of the qualities below. Then compare your notes with the class.

warmth:
patience:
goodness and kindness:

C **DISCUSSION** Talk about one or more of the questions.

  1 In what ways do you agree or disagree with Prasad's and Figueroa's ideas about beauty?

  2 Do you think the Miss Universal Beauty contest sounds better than the usual beauty contest? Why or why not?

  3 Do you think there should be beauty contests for men as well as for women? Why or why not? What in your opinion is the difference between a woman's beauty and a man's beauty?

  4 How do you explain these words in the song Prasad talks about:
  "Do you love me because I'm beautiful, or am I beautiful because you love me"?

NOW YOU CAN Define the meaning of beauty

A **NOTEPADDING** Look at the four photos. What qualities of beauty do you find in each person? Write notes.

1	Outer beauty	Inner beauty
	She has beautiful skin.	She looks warm and friendly.

1) Outer beauty

Inner beauty

2) Outer beauty

Inner beauty

3) Outer beauty

Inner beauty

4) Outer beauty

Inner beauty

B **PAIR WORK** Discuss the qualities of beauty you found in the people in the pictures. Compare your opinions. Use your notepads for support.

C **DISCUSSION** Define the meaning of beauty.

  " I think beauty is hard to describe. It's a combination of things. I consider my grandmother really beautiful because . . . "

A ▶ 3:16 Listen to the conversations. Infer what kind of product the people are discussing. Complete each statement.

1 Hawaii Bronzer is a brand of ....

2 Swan is a brand of ....

3 Truly You is a brand of ....

4 Mountain Fresh is a brand of ....

5 Silk 'n Satin is a brand of ....

6 Fresh as a Flower is a brand of ....

B Complete each statement or question.

1 There aren't (many / much) customers in the store right now.

2 Do they sell (any / many) sunscreen at the hotel gift shop? I forgot to pack some.

3 Your sister doesn't want (some / any) body lotion.

4 She doesn't wear (much / some) makeup. She doesn't need to—she has beautiful skin.

5 My son uses (any / a lot of) shaving cream.

6 There's (anyone / someone) on the phone for you. Do you want me to take a message?

7 There are (any / a lot of) salons in this neighborhood.

C Complete each statement about services at a salon or spa.

1 There's nothing like a professional .... when you're sick and tired of your beard.

2 If your hair is too long, get a ....

3 In the summer, before you wear sandals for the first time, your feet will look great if you get a ....

4 When your hands are a mess, you can get a ....

5 When your muscles are sore from too much work or exercise, a .... can help.

D Complete each conversation with the correct procedure.

1 A: I look so old! Look at my neck and my eyes.

   B: Why don't you get (a massage / a facelift)?

2 A: My back and shoulders are sore from too much exercise.

   B: They say (a chemical peel / a massage) can really help.

3 A: Look at this! I'm getting bald!

   B: Have you thought about (liposuction / hair restoration)?

WRITING

Re-read the letters on page 56. Choose one letter and write a response, using your own opinion and making your own suggestions. Explain what you think is OK or appropriate for men and women.

WRITING BOOSTER p. 147
• Writing a formal letter
• Guidance for this writing exercise

For additional language practice . . .

♫ TOP NOTCH POP • Lyrics p. 153
"Piece of Cake"

DIGITAL SONG   DIGITAL KARAOKE

ORAL REVIEW

CONTEST Look at the picture for a minute, and then close your books. With a partner, try to remember all the products and services in the picture. The pair who remembers the most products and services wins.

PAIR WORK

1 Create a conversation between the client and the clerk at the front desk of the salon. Start like this:

Hi. I have a 2:30 appointment for . . .

2 Create a conversation for the man and woman waiting for salon services. For example:

What are you here for?

✓ NOW I CAN

☐ Ask for something in a store.
☐ Make an appointment at a salon or spa.
☐ Discuss ways to improve appearance.
☐ Define the meaning of beauty.

Reference Charts

PRONUNCIATION TABLE

Vowels

Symbol	Key Words
i	beat, feed
ɪ	bit, did
eɪ	date, paid
ɛ	bet, bed
æ	bat, bad
ɑ	box, odd, father
ɔ	bought, dog
oʊ	boat, road
ʊ	book, good
u	boot, food, flu
ʌ	but, mud, mother
ə	banana, among
ɚ	shirt, murder
aɪ	bite, cry, buy, eye
aʊ	about, how
ɔɪ	voice, boy
ɪr	deer
ɛr	bare
ɑr	bar
ɔr	door
ʊr	tour

Consonants

Symbol	Key Words	Symbol	Key Words
p	pack, happy	z	zip, please, goes
b	back, rubber	ʃ	ship, machine, station, special, discussion
t	tie	ʒ	measure, vision
d	die	h	hot, who
k	came, key, quick	m	men
g	game, guest	n	sun, know, pneumonia
tʃ	church, nature, watch	ŋ	sung, ringing
dʒ	judge, general, major	w	wet, white
f	fan, photograph	l	light, long
v	van	r	right, wrong
θ	thing, breath	y	yes
ð	then, breathe		
s	sip, city, psychology		
t̬	butter, bottle		
tˀ	button		

IRREGULAR VERBS

base form	simple past	past participle	base form	simple past	past participle
be	was / were	been	leave	left	left
become	became	become	let	let	let
begin	began	begun	lose	lost	lost
break	broke	broken	make	made	made
bring	brought	brought	mean	meant	meant
build	built	built	meet	met	met
buy	bought	bought	pay	paid	paid
catch	caught	caught	put	put	put
choose	chose	chosen	quit	quit	quit
come	came	come	read /rid/	read /rɛd/	read /rɛd/
cost	cost	cost	ride	rode	ridden
cut	cut	cut	ring	rang	rung
do	did	done	rise	rose	risen
draw	drew	drawn	run	ran	run
dream	dreamed / dreamt	dreamed / dreamt	say	said	said
drink	drank	drunk	see	saw	seen
drive	drove	driven	sell	sold	sold
eat	ate	eaten	send	sent	sent
fall	fell	fallen	shake	shook	shaken
feed	fed	fed	sing	sang	sung
feel	felt	felt	sit	sat	sat
fight	fought	fought	sleep	slept	slept
find	found	found	speak	spoke	spoken
fit	fit	fit	spend	spent	spent
fly	flew	flown	stand	stood	stood
forget	forgot	forgotten	steal	stole	stolen
get	got	gotten	swim	swam	swum
give	gave	given	take	took	taken
go	went	gone	teach	taught	taught
grow	grew	grown	tell	told	told
have	had	had	think	thought	thought
hear	heard	heard	throw	threw	thrown
hit	hit	hit	understand	understood	understood
hold	held	held	wake up	woke up	woken up
hurt	hurt	hurt	wear	wore	worn
keep	kept	kept	win	won	won
know	knew	known	write	wrote	written

VERB TENSE REVIEW: PRESENT, PAST, AND FUTURE

1 THE PRESENT OF <u>BE</u>

Statements

I	am	
You We They	are	late.
He She It	is	

2 THE SIMPLE PRESENT TENSE

Statements

I You We They	speak English.
He She	speaks English.

<u>Yes</u> / <u>no</u> questions

Do	I you we they	know them?
Does	he she	eat meat?

Short answers

Yes,	I you we they	do.
	he she it	does.

No,	I you we they	don't.
	he she it	doesn't.

Information questions

What do	you we they	need?
When does	he she it	start?
Who	wants needs likes	this book?

3 THE PRESENT CONTINUOUS

Statements

I	am	watching TV.
You We They	are	studying English.
He She It	is	arriving now.

<u>Yes</u> / <u>no</u> questions

Am	I	
Are	you we they	going too fast?
Is	he she it	

Short answers

Yes,	I	am.
	you	are.
	he she it	is.
	we they	are.

No,	I'm not.
	you aren't / you're not.
	he isn't / he's not.
	she isn't / she's not.
	it isn't / it's not.
	we aren't / we're not.
	they aren't / they're not.

Information questions

What	are	you we they	doing?
When	is	he she it	leaving?
Where	am	I	staying tonight?
Who	is		driving?

4 THE PAST OF <u>BE</u>

Statements

I He She It	was late.
We You They	were early.

(The past of be*—continued)*

Yes / no questions

Was	I he she it	on time?
Were	we you they	in the same class?

Short answers

Yes,	I he she it	was.
	we you they	were.

No,	I he she it	wasn't.
	we you they	weren't.

Information questions

Where	were	we? you? they?
When	was	he she it here?
Who	were	they?
Who	was	he? she? it?

5 THE SIMPLE PAST TENSE

Many verbs are irregular in the simple past tense.
See the list of irregular verbs on page 123.

Statements

I You He She It We They	stopped working.

I You He She It We They	didn't start again.

Yes / no questions

Did	I you he she it we they	make a good dinner?

Short answers

Yes,	I you he she it we they	did.

No,	I you he she it we they	didn't.

Information questions

When did	I you he she it we they	read that?
Who		called?

6 THE FUTURE WITH BE GOING TO

Statements

I'm You're He's She's It's We're They're	going to	be here soon.

I'm You're He's She's It's We're They're	not going to	be here soon.

Yes / no questions

Are	you we they	going to want coffee?
Am	I	going to be late?
Is	he she it	going to arrive on time?

Short answers

Yes,	I	am.
	you	are.
	he she it	is.
	we they	are.

No,	I'm not. you aren't / you're not. he isn't / he's not. she isn't / she's not. it isn't / it's not. we aren't / we're not. they aren't / they're not.

Information questions

What	are	you we they	going to see?
When	is	he she it	going to shop?
Where	am	I	going to stay tomorrow?
Who	is		going to call?

TOP NOTCH 2A

Grammar Booster

Grammar Booster

The Grammar Booster is optional. It offers a variety of information and extra practice. Sometimes it further explains or expands the unit grammar and points out common errors. In other cases, it reviews and practices previously learned grammar that would be helpful when learning new grammar concepts. If you use the Grammar Booster, you will find extra exercises in the Workbook in a separate section labeled Grammar Booster. The Grammar Booster content is not tested on any *Top Notch* tests.

 **Lesson 1**

The present perfect: information questions

Form information questions by inverting <u>have</u> and the subject of the sentence.
What **have** you **seen** in Paris?
What (OR Which) countries **have** you **visited**?
Where **has** she **gone** scuba diving?
How **have** your parents **been**?
How many cities **have** you **visited** this week?
Who **have** you **traveled** with?

Note: When <u>Who</u> is the subject of the sentence, there is no inversion.
Who **has traveled** to Miami in the last two months?

On a separate sheet of paper, write information questions. Use the present perfect.

1 what dishes / she / try / in Mérida
2 who / you / invite / to the party
3 where / he / work / before
4 which movies / they / see
5 how / your children / be
6 who / climb / Grouse Mountain
7 what / they / hear / about the new school
8 how many times / she / take / that class

UNIT 1 *Lesson 2*

The present perfect: use and placement of <u>yet</u> and <u>already</u>

Remember: Use <u>yet</u> or <u>already</u> in questions.
Have you read the book **yet**? OR Have you **already** read the book?

Use <u>already</u> in affirmative statements. Place <u>already</u> before the main verb or at the end of the statement.
I've **already** read the book. OR I've read the book **already**.

Use <u>yet</u> in negative statements. Place <u>yet</u> at the end of the statement or between <u>have</u> and the base form.
I haven't read the book **yet**. OR I haven't **yet** read the book.

Be careful!
Don't use <u>yet</u> in affirmative statements. Don't use <u>already</u> in negative statements.
DON'T SAY Yes, I've read the book ~~yet~~. / No, I haven't ~~already~~ read the book.

Don't use <u>ever</u> with <u>yet</u> or <u>already</u>.
DON'T SAY Have you ~~ever~~ read the book ~~yet~~? / Have you ~~ever~~ read the book ~~already~~?

A On a separate sheet of paper, rewrite each statement or question, using <u>already</u> or <u>yet</u>.

1 (yet) Has she finished the homework?
2 (yet) They haven't seen the movie.
3 (already) We've tried fried clams several times.
4 (already) Has your father left?

B On a separate sheet of paper, rewrite each sentence, using <u>already</u> or <u>yet</u>.

1 I haven't had dinner.
2 She's been to London, Berlin, and Rome.
3 They haven't called home.
4 We've finished our class.

The present perfect: *ever*, *never*, and *before*

Use <u>ever</u> in questions. Use <u>never</u> in negative statements and short answers. Do not use <u>ever</u> in affirmative statements.

Have you **ever** made sushi?

Yes, I have. OR Yes, I've made sushi. NOT Yes, I've ~~ever~~ made sushi.

No, I **never** have. OR No, I've **never** made sushi.

You can also use <u>before</u> in negative statements with <u>never</u>.

I've **never** been to Thailand **before**.

In very informal speech, <u>ever</u> is sometimes used with <u>never</u> for strong emphasis. This meaning of <u>ever</u> is similar to "in my whole life."

I've **never ever** seen a Charlie Chaplin movie.

C   On a separate sheet of paper, answer each question, using real information. If the answer is <u>yes</u>, write when this happened.

1 Have you ever gone on a cruise?

2 Have you ever tried Indian food?

3 Have you ever been to Hawaii?

4 Have you ever met a famous person?

5 Have you ever fallen in love?

6 Have you ever played golf?

UNIT 2 *Lesson 1*

The present perfect and the present perfect continuous: unfinished (or continuing) actions

Unfinished (or continuing) actions are those that began in the past, continue in the present, and may possibly continue into the future. Here are three ways to talk about unfinished actions:

1 the present perfect with <u>since</u>: Use <u>since</u> with a stated start time in the past.

I've lived here **since** 2001. (2001 is the stated start time. I still live here, so the action "continues.")

2 the present perfect with <u>for</u>: Use <u>for</u> to describe the period of time from its start until the present.

I've lived here **for** five years. (Emphasis is on the five-year period. I still live here, so the action "continues.")

3 the present perfect continuous with <u>for</u> or <u>since</u>: Form the present perfect continuous with the present perfect of <u>be</u> and a present participle.

I've **been living** here since 2001. OR I've **been living** here for five years. (In both cases, the action "continues.")

When describing unfinished or continuing actions with <u>for</u> and <u>since</u>, the present perfect and the present perfect continuous are both correct. Some people feel the present perfect continuous emphasizes the continuing time a bit more.

A   Read the sentences with the present perfect. Check each sentence that describes an unfinished or continuing action.

☐ 1 The Pitts have lived in China since the late nineties.

☐ 2 Carmen has been living in Buenos Aires since last year.

☐ 3 I've visited Paris three times.

☐ 4 Ted has been visiting Paris since 2005.

☐ 5 We have eaten in that great Indian restaurant for years.

☐ 6 They've eaten in that Indian restaurant before.

☐ 7 My brother has been playing tennis for many years.

☐ 8 Min-ji has played tennis twice.

B   Complete each statement with the present perfect continuous.

1 *Rio* .... (play) at the Children's Classics Cinema every Saturday since 2010.

2 Robert .... (wait) in the ticket holders' line for a pretty long time.

3 People .... (worry about) violence in movies since the sixties.

4 I'.. (talk about) that movie for weeks.

5 We'.. (come) to this classics movie theater for two years.

Spelling rules for the present participle: review

Add -ing to the base form of the verb
speak ➔ speaking

If the base form ends in a silent -e, drop the -e and add -ing.
have ➔ having

In verbs of one syllable, if the last three letters are a consonant-vowel-consonant (C-V-C) series, double the last consonant and then add -ing.
C V C
s i t ➔ sitting

Be careful! Don't double the last consonant in words that end in -w, -x, or -y.
flow ➔ flowing
fix ➔ fixing
pay ➔ paying

In verbs of more than one syllable that end in a consonant-vowel-consonant series, double the last consonant only if the stress is on the last syllable.

con • trol ➔ controlling   BUT   or • der ➔ ordering

C   Write the present participle for these base forms.

1 find	8 go	15 come	22 forget	29 begin ....
2 be	9 make	16 leave	23 eat	30 tell ....
3 lose	10 fix	17 drive	24 pay	31 bring ....
4 put	11 know	18 meet	25 stand	32 take ....
5 get	12 speak	19 blow	26 think	
6 say	13 hear	20 give	27 buy	
7 write	14 let	21 run	28 see	

UNIT 2   Lesson 2

Like, want, would like, would rather: review and expansion; common errors

Use like and want + a direct object to express likes, dislikes, and desires.
They like documentaries. We don't like science fiction.
She wants a ticket to the late show.

Use would like + a direct object to make a polite offer or a request.
A: Would you like tickets for *Casablanca*?
B: Yes, please. We'd like two tickets for the 8:00 show.

Use would like + an infinitive (to + base form) to make a polite offer or to express wants.
Would you like to stream a movie on your tablet?
Where would you like to go?
I'd like to download a movie onto my tablet.
She'd like to see a comedy.

Use would rather + a base form to express a preference for an activity.
A: Would you like to see the movie downtown or at the theater in the mall?
B: I'd rather see it at the mall.

Use than with would rather to contrast preferences.
I'd rather stream a movie than go to the theater.
They'd rather go to a Woody Allen film than a Martin Scorsese film.

Be careful!
Don't use a base form after would like.
My friends would like to meet in front of the theater. NOT My friends ~~would like meet~~ in front of the theater.

Don't use an infinitive after would rather.
We'd rather get tickets for the early show. NOT We'd rather ~~to get~~ tickets for the early show.

A On a separate sheet of paper, write sentences and questions using these words and phrases.

1 They / would like / see / the Woody Allen film.
2 What time / you / would rather / meet?
3 Who / would like / order / eggs for breakfast?
4 they / rather / Would / watch TV or go out?
5 Jason / would like / have / a large container of popcorn.
6 I'd rather / rent / a sci-fi film tonight.
7 Her parents / rather / not / watch / anything too violent.
8 Who'd rather / not / see / that silly animated film?

B Correct the errors in these sentences.

1 I would rather to stay home than to go out.
2 She would like buy a ticket to tonight's show.
3 My friends would like download movies from the Internet.
4 Would they rather to see an animated film than an action film?
5 Do they rather see movies at home?
6 Who would like go to the late show tonight?
7 My husband likes two tickets to the concert.

C On a separate sheet of paper, answer each question in a complete sentence, expressing your own preference.

1 What genre of movie do you usually like?
2 What movie do you want to see this weekend?
3 What would you like to have for dinner tonight?
4 Would you rather see a comedy or a horror film?
5 Would you like to rent a DVD or go to the movies?

UNIT 3 — Lesson 1

Will: expansion

Will and be going to
Use will or be going to for predictions about the future. The meaning is the same.
It'll rain tomorrow. = It's going to rain tomorrow.

Use be going to, NOT will, when you already have a plan for the future.
A: Are you going to come to class tomorrow?
B: No. I'm going to go to the beach instead. NOT No. I'll go to the beach instead.

Other uses of will
Use will, NOT be going to, to talk about the immediate future when you do not already have a plan.
Maybe I'll go to the beach this weekend. NOT Maybe I'm going to go to the beach this weekend.

Use will, NOT be going to, to express willingness.
I'll pay for Internet service, but I won't pay for the airport shuttle. (= I'm willing to pay for Internet service, but I'm not willing to pay for the airport shuttle.)

Can, should, and have to: future meaning
Can and should are modals and should never be used with will.

You can use can alone to express future possibility.
Tomorrow morning you can ask the hotel for a rollaway bed.
They can't go to the museum tomorrow. It's closed on Mondays.

You can use should alone to express future advice.
You should visit the Empire State Building next week. It's great.

However, you can use will with have to + a base form to express future obligation.
I'll have to leave the 2:00 meeting early.
We won't have to make a reservation at a restaurant tonight.

A On a separate sheet of paper, write five sentences about your plans for the weekend, using be going to. Then write the sentences again, using will.

B   On a separate sheet of paper, write five sentences with <u>will</u> or <u>won't</u> for willingness
    on one of the following topics.

> **Topics**
> - kinds of exercise you're willing (or not willing) to do
> - kinds of food you're willing (or not willing) to eat for breakfast
> - kinds of clothes you're willing (or not willing) to wear

C   Complete the sentences, using <u>will</u> or <u>won't</u> with <u>have to</u>.

1   .... (she / have to / call) the office before 6:00.
2   .... (they / have to / reserve) their tickets by Monday.
3   .... (we / not have to / cancel) the meeting if Mr. Carson's flight is on time.
4   .... (I / have to / leave) a message for my boss.
5   .... (you / not have to / order) room service if you arrive before 10:00 P.M.
6   .... (we / have to / take) a taxi to the airport.

UNIT 3   Lesson 2

The real conditional: present

Use the present real conditional to express general and scientific facts. Use the simple present tense or the present tense of <u>be</u> in both clauses.
    If it rains, flights are late. [fact]
    If you heat water to 100 degrees, it boils. [scientific fact]

In present real conditional sentences, when (or whenever) is often used instead of <u>if</u>.
    When (or Whenever) it rains, flights are late.
    When (or Whenever) you heat water to 100 degrees, it boils.

A   On a separate sheet of paper, write present real conditional sentences.

1   Water (freeze) when you (lower) its temperature below zero degrees.
2   Whenever my daughter (take) her umbrella to school, she (forget) to bring it home.
3   She (go) on vacation every August if she (not have) too much work.
4   He (run) in the park if the weather (be) dry.
5   In my company, if cashiers (make) a mistake, they (repay) the money.

The real conditional: future

Use the future real conditional to express what you believe will happen in the future under certain conditions or as a result of certain actions. Use the simple present tense or the present of <u>be</u> in the <u>if</u> clause. Use a future form (<u>will</u> or <u>be going to</u>) in the result clause.
    If I go to sleep too late tonight, I won't be able to get up on time. (future condition, future result)
    If she comes home after 8:00, I'm not going to make dinner. (future condition, future result)

Remember: Use a comma when the <u>if</u> clause comes first. Don't use a comma when the <u>if</u> clause comes at the end of the sentence.
    If I see him, I'll tell her.   I'll tell her if I see him.

Be careful! Don't use a future form in the <u>if</u> clause.
    If I see him, I'll tell her. NOT If I ~~will see~~ him, I'll tell her. NOT If I'~~m going to see~~ him, I'll tell her.

B   Circle the correct form to complete each future real conditional sentence.

1   If they (like / will like) the movie, they (see / will see) it again.
2   I ('m going to talk / talk) to her if she (does / 's going to do) that again.
3   If you (buy / are going to buy) some eggs, I (make / 'll make) you an omelet tonight.
4   If they (see / will see) her tomorrow, they (drive / 'll drive) her home.
5   (Are you going to study / Do you study) Italian if they (offer / will offer) it next year?

C   On a separate sheet of paper, complete each future real conditional sentence with true information. Use a comma when the <u>if</u> clause comes first.

1 If I live to be 100 . . .
2 My family will be angry if . . .
3 If I don't practice English every day . . .
4 If I go to my favorite restaurant next week . . .
5 I'll buy a new smart phone if . . .
6 If I need new shoes . . .

UNIT 4 Lesson 1

The past continuous: expansion

The past continuous describes an action that was continuous until (and possibly after) the moment at which another action took place. The words <u>when</u> or <u>while</u> are often used in sentences that contrast continuing and completed actions.

He was talking on the phone when the storm began. (continuous action, then completed action)
While I was living in Chile, I got married. (continuous action, then completed action)

The past continuous also describes two continuing actions occurring in the same period of time.

While she was driving, her husband was reading the newspaper.
They were eating, and the music was playing.

On a separate sheet of paper, use the prompts to write logical sentences. Use the past continuous and the simple past tense in each sentence.

1 She / take a test at school / when / she / hear the fire alarm
2 While I / talk to my mother on the phone / the TV show / start
3 Mr. Park / cook dinner / when / Mrs. Park / finish the laundry
4 Mr. Kemp / work in the garden / when / the rain / begin
5 While / Claudia / pick up / their rental car / Alex / call / their hotel
6 While / Nancy / shop at the grocery store / she / see / an old friend

UNIT 4 Lesson 2

Nouns and pronouns: review

A <u>noun</u> is a word that names a person, a place, or a thing. Nouns are either common or proper. A proper noun is capitalized.

common nouns: car, windshield, doctor, woman, father
proper nouns: Martin, Caracas, Carla's Restaurant

Two functions of nouns in sentences are subjects and direct objects. The subject performs the action of the verb. The object receives the action.

subject	direct object
Carla's Restaurant serves breakfast all day long.	

A <u>pronoun</u> is a word that represents or replaces a noun. Pronouns also function as subjects and direct objects.

subject pronouns: I, you, he, she, it, we, they
object pronouns: me, you, him, her, it, us, them

subject		direct object	
My parents	drove	the car	to the airport.
They		it	

First, underline the subjects and circle the objects in these sentences. Then label each noun as either "common" or "proper." Finally, put a check (✓) above each pronoun. (Note: Not every sentence contains a pronoun.)

proper   *common*
Italians drive fast (cars.)

1 We love big vans.
2 The children broke the side-view mirror.
3 Ms. Workman picked up the car this morning.
4 Rand loves sports cars, and his wife loves them, too.

5 A man driving a sports car hit our minivan.
6 I returned the rental car at the airport.
7 A-1 Rental Agency called me about the reservation.

UNIT 5 Lesson 1

Some and any: review

Some and **any** are indefinite quantifiers. They indicate an indefinite number or amount.
There are some toothbrushes in aisle 2. (We don't know how many.)
They are buying some shaving cream. (We don't know how much.)
Could I get some nail files? (We're not asking for a specific number of nail files.)
Do they have any makeup in this store? (We're not asking specifically how much.)

Be careful to use some and any correctly with count and non-count nouns:
Some: with non-count nouns and plural count nouns in affirmative statements
       non-count noun   plural count noun
We need some sunscreen and some combs. They have some here.
Any: with non-count nouns and plural count nouns in negative statements
          non-count noun   plural count noun
A: She doesn't want any shampoo, and he doesn't need any nail clippers.
B: Good! We don't have to buy any, then. I'm out of cash.
Any or some: with count and non-count nouns in questions
Do they need any toothpaste or sunscreen for the trip?
Do we need any razors or toothbrushes?

> **Remember:** Count nouns name things you can count individually. They have singular and plural forms (1 nail file, 3 combs). Non-count nouns name things you cannot count individually. They don't have plural forms. Use containers, quantifiers, and other modifiers to make non-count nouns countable.
>
> a bottle of shampoo / aftershave
> a tube of toothpaste / lipstick
> a bar of soap
> a can of hairspray / deodorant / shaving cream
> 250 milliliters of sunscreen

A On a separate sheet of paper, change these sentences from affirmative to negative. Follow the example.

There is some shampoo in the shower. *There isn't any shampoo in the shower.*

1 There are some razors next to the sink.
2 We have some nail clippers.
3 They need some brushes for the children.
4 She's buying some mascara.

5 The manicurists need some new nail polish.
6 I want some sunscreen on my back.
7 There is some dental floss in aisle 4.
8 They need some deodorant for the trip.

B Complete each sentence with some or any.

1 I don't need .... more hand lotion.
2 There isn't .... makeup in the bag.
3 We don't see .... scissors in the whole store.
4 They need .... soap to wash their hands.

5 It's too bad that there isn't .... toothpaste.
6 I don't see .... combs or brushes on those shelves.
7 I know I had .... nail files in my bag. Now I can't find them.

Too many, too much, and enough

The word <u>too</u> indicates a quantity that is excessive—more than someone wants or needs. Use <u>enough</u> to indicate that a quantity or amount is satisfactory.

Use <u>too many</u> and <u>not too many</u> for count nouns.
There are too many customers waiting in line.

Use <u>too much</u> and <u>not too much</u> for non-count nouns.
There's too much toothpaste on the toothbrush.

Use <u>enough</u> and <u>not enough</u> for both count and non-count nouns.
There's enough shampoo, but there aren't enough razors.

C Complete each sentence with <u>too many</u>, <u>too much</u>, or <u>enough</u>.

1 Let's do our nails. Do we have .... nail polish for both of us?

2 This shampoo has .... perfume. It smells awful!

3 It's not a good idea to buy .... fruit. We're not going to be home for a few days.

4 This menu has .... choices. I can't make up my mind.

5 Check the bathroom shelf to see if we have .... soap. Mom and Dad are coming to visit.

6 I don't like when there are .... brands. I can't decide which one to buy.

7 There's no way to get a haircut today. .... people had the same idea!

8 They don't want to spend .... money on makeup. They're trying to save money.

Comparative quantifiers <u>fewer</u> and <u>less</u>

Use <u>fewer</u> for count nouns. Use <u>less</u> for non-count nouns.
The Cosmetique store has fewer brands of makeup than the Emporium.
There's less shampoo in this bottle than in that tube.

D Complete each sentence with <u>fewer</u> or <u>less</u>.

1 Which class has .... students—the early class or the late one?

2 The recipe calls for .... cheese than I thought.

3 It has .... ingredients, too.

4 Don't rent from Cars Plus. They have .... kinds of cars than International.

5 The Cineplus has .... movies this weekend than usual.

6 Is there .... body lotion in the small size or the economy size?

UNIT 5 *Lesson 2*

Indefinite pronouns: <u>something</u>, <u>anything</u>, <u>everything</u>, and <u>nothing</u>

Use <u>something</u>, <u>nothing</u>, or <u>everything</u> in affirmative statements.
There's something in this box.
Nothing can convince me to get a pedicure.
Everything is ready.

Use <u>anything</u> in negative statements.
There isn't anything in the fridge.

Use <u>something</u>, <u>anything</u>, or <u>everything</u> in <u>yes</u> / <u>no</u> questions.
Is there something we should talk about? Is anything wrong?
Do you have everything you need?

<u>Nothing</u> has the same meaning as <u>not anything</u>. Don't use <u>nothing</u> in negative statements.
There isn't anything in the fridge. = There's nothing in the fridge. NOT There isn't nothing in the fridge.

Choose the correct indefinite pronoun to complete each sentence.

1 I need to go to the store to buy (something / anything).
2 There is (something / anything) I can do to help.
3 There isn't (everything / anything) you can do to make yourself taller.
4 I went on the Internet to find (something / anything) about how to use sunscreen.
5 They have (something / anything) that helps you lose weight.
6 There's (anything / nothing) that can make you look young again.
7 They can't get (anything / nothing) to eat there after ten o'clock.

TOP NOTCH 2A

Writing Booster

Writing Booster

The Writing Booster is optional. It is intended to teach students the conventions of written English. Each unit's Writing Booster is focused both on a skill and its application to the Writing exercise from the Unit Review page.

UNIT 1 Avoiding run-on sentences

An independent clause is a sentence with a subject and a verb.

subject	verb
I	saw a photo of the mountain.
It	looked very high.

In writing, don't combine independent clauses without using a coordinating conjunction, such as <u>and</u> or <u>but</u>.

Run-on sentence ✗ I saw a photo of the mountain it looked very high.

Correct a run-on sentence by (a) using a period to separate it into two sentences, or (b) using a coordinating conjunction to combine the two independent clauses. A comma before the conjunction is optional.

✓ I saw a photo of the mountain. It looked very high.
✓ I saw a photo of the mountain, and it looked very high.

Be careful! Do not use a comma to combine independent clauses. Use a period to separate them.

Run-on sentence ✗ A new student arrived yesterday, he is from Santos.
✓ A new student arrived yesterday. He is from Santos.

> **Remember:** A sentence begins with a capital letter and ends with a period.

A Write ✗ if the item contains a run-on sentence. Write ✓ if the item is written correctly.

☐ 1 Ann is Canadian she doesn't speak French.
☐ 2 They're good students they work very hard.
☐ 3 My brother is a lawyer, he lives in Hong Kong.
☐ 4 Victor and Lisa came home late last night. They stayed up until 4:00 A.M.
☐ 5 Some people think cities are beautiful I don't agree.
☐ 6 I have been to three foreign countries, I have never been to the United States.
☐ 7 We haven't tried Polish food, but we have tried Hungarian food.
☐ 8 I have never been to the top of the Empire State Building in New York, I have been to the top of Taipei 101 in Taipei.
☐ 9 I visited Jeju in Korea, and it was really beautiful.

B On a separate sheet of paper, write each of the run-on sentences in Exercise A correctly.

C Guidance for the Writing Exercise (on page 12) After you write about your interesting experience, check carefully to see if you have written any run-on sentences. Use a period to separate the independent clauses, or use the coordinating conjunctions <u>and</u> or <u>but</u> to combine them.

indent ——————→ [   ]Before the 1960s, most movies did not show much graphic violence. When fighting or shooting occurred on the screen, it was clean: Bang! You're dead! The victim fell to the ground and died, perhaps after speaking a few final words. The viewer never saw blood or suffering. But in the late 1960s, filmmakers such as Arthur Penn and Sam Peckinpah began making movies with more graphic violence, such as *Bonnie and Clyde* and *The Wild Bunch*. They believed that if audiences could see how truly horrible real violence was, people would be less violent in their own lives.

Today, special-effects technology has made it possible to create very realistic images of bloodshed and violence. Steven Prince, author of *Savage Cinema: Sam Peckinpah and the Rise of Ultraviolent Movies*, describes the difference between early movies and the movies of today: ". . . filmmakers can create any image that they can dream up." So, Prince believes, because of technology, movies today are more and more violent and bloody.

A paragraph is a group of sentences that relate to a topic or a theme. When your writing contains sections about a variety of topics, it is a good idea to divide it into separate paragraphs.

When there is more than one paragraph, it is customary, though not required, to include **a topic sentence** in each paragraph that summarizes or announces the main idea of the paragraph. The other sentences in the paragraph traditionally include details or facts that support the main idea. Using topic sentences makes paragraphs clearer and easier to understand.

In the writing model to the right, there are two paragraphs, each beginning with a topic sentence (highlighted in yellow).

In the first paragraph, the topic sentence informs us that the paragraph will contain details about violence in movies "before the 1960s."

In the second paragraph, the topic sentence informs us that the paragraph will shift focus. The word "Today" lets the reader know what the focus of the paragraph will be.

Without the topic sentences, the ideas would run together and be difficult to follow.

Remember: Indent the first word of each new paragraph so readers know that a new section of the writing is beginning.

A   Choose a topic sentence for each paragraph.

1

_____ . Some people are worried that viewing a lot of violence in movies and video games can be dangerous. They feel that it can make violence seem normal and can cause people to imitate the violent behavior, doing the same thing themselves. Other people disagree. They believe that showing violence is honest and can even be helpful.

a Many people say violence in movies can be harmful.
b People have different opinions about how violence can affect viewers.
c People imitate violent behavior they see in movies.

2

_____ . This 1967 Arthur Penn movie is about a real gang of violent bank robbers who terrorized the U.S. Southwest in the 1930s. Bonnie (Faye Dunaway) and Clyde (Warren Beatty), and their gang were believed to be responsible for thirteen deaths and many robberies before they were finally killed.

a *Bonnie and Clyde* is based on a true story.
b Arthur Penn is one of the most famous directors of the 1960s.
c There were a lot of bank robberies in the 1930s.

3

_____ . The U.S. documentary *Spellbound* visits the homes of eight finalists for the National Spelling Bee and then follows them to the finals in Washington, D.C. We get to know the kids and their families.

a Spelling bees are popular in the U.S., and there have been a number of them in Washington.
b The finals of the National Spelling Bee take place in Washington, D.C.
c Some documentaries give us an intimate view of people and their lives.

B   On a separate sheet of paper, write two paragraphs of three to five sentences each with details about the following topics. Make sure you have included a topic sentence for each paragraph that summarizes or announces the main idea of the paragraph.

Paragraph 1	Paragraph 2
The story of a time you (or others) were late to meet someone for an event	The story of what you (or the others) did after the event

C   Guidance for the Writing Exercise (on page 24) On the notepad, write notes about why some people think watching violence is harmful and why others think it isn't. Use your notes as a guide for your paragraphs about violence. Include a topic sentence for each paragraph to summarize the main ideas.

Harmful:

Not harmful:

UNIT 3   Avoiding sentence fragments with <u>because</u> or <u>since</u>

Remember: You can use the subordinating conjunctions <u>because</u> or <u>since</u> to give a reason. <u>Because</u> and <u>since</u> answer a <u>Why</u> question. A clause that begins with <u>because</u> or <u>since</u> is called a dependent clause. A dependent clause gives information about an independent clause.

—— independent clause ——   —————— dependent clause ——————
I prefer the Hotel Casablanca   because (or since) it looks very interesting.

A dependent clause with <u>because</u> or <u>since</u> can also come at the beginning of a sentence. If it comes first, use a comma.

Because it looks very interesting, I prefer the Hotel Casablanca.

In writing, a dependent clause alone is an error called a "sentence fragment." It is not a sentence because it does not express a complete idea.

Sentence fragment   ✗ I prefer the Hotel Casablanca. ~~Because it looks very interesting.~~

To correct a sentence fragment with <u>because</u> or <u>since</u>, make sure it is combined with an independent clause. Or rewrite the sentence without <u>because</u> or <u>since</u> to create an independent clause.

✓ I prefer the Hotel Casablanca because it looks very interesting.
✓ I prefer the Hotel Casablanca. It looks very interesting.

A   In the following paragraph, underline four sentence fragments with <u>because</u> or <u>since</u>.

> When I was a child, I had three very important dreams. Because I was young, I thought they would all come true. The first one was that I wanted to be an architect. Because I loved modern buildings. Since I wanted to help people. The second dream was to be a doctor. The last one was to be a flight attendant. Since I liked to travel. Only one of my dreams became a reality. I am an architect today. Because I really love my job. I think it was really the right choice for me.

B   On a separate sheet of paper, write the paragraph again. Correct all the sentence fragments. Combine the dependent clauses with independent clauses to make complete sentences.

C   Guidance for the Writing Exercise (on page 36) In your paragraph about a hotel, include at least three reasons using <u>because</u> or <u>since</u>. Then check carefully to make sure that there are no sentence fragments.

UNIT 4   And, In addition, Furthermore, and Therefore

And
And connects two or more words in a series. Use commas to separate words when there are more than two in the series. (The last comma is optional.)

I'm concerned about **aggressive and inattentive** driving. (no comma: <u>and</u> connects two adjectives.)

Inattentive drivers sometimes **eat and talk** on their cell phones while they are driving. (no comma: <u>and</u> connects two verbs with the same subject.)

Gesturing, staring, and multitasking are three things aggressive drivers often do. (A comma is necessary: <u>and</u> connects more than two words in a series. The comma after <u>staring</u> is optional.)

<u>And</u> can also combine two separate complete sentences into one sentence. In the new sentence, the two original sentences are called "independent clauses." The comma is common but optional.

——————— complete sentence ——————— —— complete sentence ——
Aggressive drivers do many dangerous things. They cause a lot of crashes.

——————— independent clause ——————— —— independent clause ——
Aggressive drivers do many dangerous things, **and** they cause a lot of crashes.

A   Insert commas where necessary or optional in the sentences.

1 She enjoys swimming hiking and fishing.
2 I don't like SUVs and other large cars.
3 We're traveling to France Italy and Spain.
4 Marianne and Sally are coming with us.
5 I'm renting a car and I'm driving it to Chicago.
6 This agency has nice convertibles vans and sports cars.

B   On a separate sheet of paper, combine each pair of sentences into one sentence consisting of two independent clauses. Use <u>and</u>.

1 They made a call to a car rental company. They reserved a minivan for the weekend.
2 The left front headlight is broken. It won't turn on.
3 We rented a full-size sedan with a sunroof. We opened it because the weather was beautiful.
4 I hit the car in front of me. A passenger in the back seat was hurt.
5 You can drop the car off at nine o'clock. You can pick it up in the late afternoon.

In addition, Furthermore, and Therefore
Use <u>In addition</u> and <u>Furthermore</u> to add to the ideas in a previous sentence. <u>In addition</u> and <u>Furthermore</u> are approximately equal in meaning, but <u>Furthermore</u> is a little more formal. You can use both in the same writing to avoid repetition.

People should pay attention to their own driving. **In addition**, they should be aware of the driving of others.

I think defensive driving makes sense. **Furthermore**, it has been proven to reduce the number of accidents.

Use <u>therefore</u> to introduce a result.

——————————————————— result ———————————————————
Ron has had a lot of accidents. **Therefore**, the rental company said he couldn't rent one of their cars.

Note: It's customary to use a comma after <u>In addition</u>, <u>Furthermore</u>, and <u>Therefore</u>.

C   Complete the statements with <u>In addition</u> or <u>Therefore</u>.

1 The other driver was speeding. _____ , she wasn't paying attention.
2 No one was hurt. _____ , we didn't have to go to the hospital after the crash.
3 I was taking a business trip with a lot of equipment. _____ , I rented a car with a lot of trunk space.
4 They need to rent a minivan for their trip to Montreal. _____ , they have to stay in a pet-friendly hotel because they plan to bring their pet dog.

D   Guidance for the Writing Exercise (on page 48) In your paragraph about good and bad drivers, use <u>And</u>, <u>In addition</u>, <u>Furthermore</u>, and <u>Therefore</u>. Then check your paragraph carefully to see if you have used commas correctly.

There aren't many rules for informal social communication such as e-mails, text messages, and handwritten social notes. There are, however, important rules and conventions for formal written communication, such as business letters, memos, and e-mails. For these, be sure to include the following elements:

- your address
- the recipient's name, position, and address
- the date
- a salutation
- a complimentary close
- your typewritten name and, in a letter or memo, your handwritten signature

Note: When business correspondence is an e-mail, it's not necessary to include addresses.

If you know the recipient's name, the salutation should use the following format: Dear [title + last name]. It's common in a formal letter to use a colon (:) after the name. In less formal letters, a comma is appropriate.

Dear Mr. Smith: Dear Marie,

If you don't know the recipient's name or gender, use this format:
Dear Sir or Madam: OR   To whom it may concern:

Follow the layout and punctuation in the writing model to the right.

your address ⎰ 657 Boulevard East
New Compton, Fortunia
e-mail: fclasson@vmail.gr

date ⎰ December 14, 2016

Manager
The Tipton Spa
Tipton Hotel   ⎰ recipient's address
2200 Byway Street
Sylvania, Sorrento

Dear Sir or Madam: ⎰ salutation

I'm writing to tell you that I was very happy with the service provided by the staff of the Tipton Spa when I was in Sylvania last week. The hair stylist gave me a wonderful haircut, and the masseur was really top notch. I particularly enjoyed the relaxing music that played over the public address system. Finally, the prices were fair, and I left the spa feeling great.

I want you to know that I am recommending the Tipton Spa to all my friends and have told them that they should visit you even if they are staying in another hotel or if they are in Sylvania for the day. In fact, I have told them that it's worth traveling to Sylvania just to visit the spa. Congratulations on such a wonderful spa.

Sincerely, ⎰ complimentary close
Francine Classon ⎰ signature
Francine Classon ⎰ typewritten name

Other common complimentary closes
Cordially,
Sincerely yours,
Best regards,

A Think of a business, such as a hotel, a store, a salon, a gym, or a restaurant where you have received good service. On the notepad, write notes about the business.

Name of business:
Address:
Why you are happy with the service:

B On a separate sheet of paper, write a letter of thanks to the manager of the business in Exercise A. Explain what you like about the service. Use your notes and the writing model above as a guide.

C **Guidance for the Writing Exercise (on page 60)** Look at the letter that you chose from page 56. On the notepad below, list three methods that the writer could use to improve his or her appearance. Make notes of the advantages and disadvantages of each method. Then use your notes as a guide to help you write your response letter. Be sure to include your name and address, the date, a salutation, and a complimentary close in your letter.

Method	Advantages	Disadvantages
1.		
2.		
3.		

Top Notch Pop Lyrics

▶ 1:16–1:17 **Greetings and Small Talk**
[Unit 1]
You look so familiar. Have we met before?
I don't think you're from around here.
It might have been two weeks ago, but I'm
not sure.
Has it been a month or a year?
I have a funny feeling that I've met you twice.
That's what they call déjà vu.
You were saying something friendly, trying to
be nice—and now you're being friendly, too.
One look, one word.
It's the friendliest sound that I've ever heard.
Thanks for your greetings.
I'm glad this meeting occurred.

(CHORUS)
Greetings and small talk
make the world go round.
On every winding road I've walked,
this is what I've found.

Have you written any letters to your friends
back home?
Have you had a chance to do that?
Have you spoken to your family on the
telephone?
Have you taken time for a chat?
Bow down, shake hands.
Do whatever you do in your native land.
I'll be happy to greet you
in any way that you understand.

(CHORUS)

Have you seen the latest movie out of
Hollywood?
Have you read about it yet?
If you haven't eaten dinner, are you in the
mood for a meal you won't forget?
Bow down, shake hands.
Do whatever you do in your native land.
I'll be happy to greet you
in any way that you understand.

(CHORUS)

▶ 1:35–1:36 **Better Late Than Never**
[Unit 2]
Where have you been? I've waited for you.
I'd rather not say how long.
The movie began one hour ago.
How did you get the time all wrong?
Well, I got stuck in traffic, and when I arrived
I couldn't find a parking place.
Did you buy the tickets? You're kidding—
for real?
Let me pay you back, in that case.

(CHORUS)
Sorry I'm late.
I know you've waited here forever.
How long has it been?
It's always better late than never.

When that kind of movie comes to the
big screen,
it always attracts a crowd,
and I've always wanted to see it with you—
but it looks like we've missed it now.
I know what you're saying, but actually,
I would rather watch a video.

So why don't we rent it and bring it
back home?
Let's get in the car and go.

(CHORUS)

Didn't you mention, when we made our
plans, that you've seen this movie recently?
It sounds so dramatic, and I'm so upset,
I'd rather see a comedy!
Well, which comedy do you recommend?
It really doesn't matter to me.
I still haven't seen 'The World and a Day'.
I've heard that one is pretty funny.

(CHORUS)

▶ 2:17–2:18 **Checking Out** **[Unit 3]**
Ms. Jones travels all alone.
She doesn't need much space—
a single room with a nice twin bed
and a place for her suitcase.
Her stay is always satisfactory,
but in the morning she's going to be
checking out.
Mr. Moon will be leaving soon,
and when he does I'll say,
"Thank you, sir, for staying with us.
How do you want to pay?"
And in the end it isn't hard.
He'll put it on his credit card. He's
checking out.
Would you like to leave a message?
Could you call back later?
Do you need some extra towels
or today's newspaper?
Can I get you anything?
Would you like room service?
I'm so sorry.
Am I making you nervous?
Good evening.
I'll ring that room for you.
Is that all?
I'll be glad to put you through.
I'm sorry, but he's not answering.
The phone just rings and rings.
The couple in room 586
have made a king-size mess.
Pick up the laundry. Turn down the beds.
We have another guest
coming with his family.
You'd better hurry or they will be
checking out. . .

▶ 2:36–2:37 **Wheels around the**
World **[Unit 4]**
Was I going too fast
or a little too slow?
I was looking out the window,
and I just don't know.
I must have turned the steering wheel
a little too far
when I drove into the bumper
of that luxury car.
Oh no!
How awful!
What a terrible day!
I'm sorry to hear that.
Are you OK?

(CHORUS)
Wheels around the World
are waiting here with your car.
Pick it up.
Turn it on.
Play the radio.
Wheels around the World—
"helping you to go far."
You can drive anywhere.
Buckle up and go.

Did I hit the red sedan,
or did it hit me?
I was talking on the cell phone
in my SUV.
Nothing was broken,
and no one was hurt,
but I did spill some coffee
on my favorite shirt.
Oh no!
Thank goodness you're still alive!
I'm so happy that
you survived.

(CHORUS)

What were you doing when you hit that tree?
I was racing down the mountain, and the
brakes failed me.
How did it happen? Was the road still wet?
Well, there might have been a danger sign,
But I forget.
The hood popped open and the door fell off.
The headlights blinked and the
engine coughed.
The side-view mirror had a terrible crack.
The gearshift broke. Can I bring the
car back?
Oh no!
Thank goodness
you're still alive!
I'm so happy that
you survived.

(CHORUS)

▶ 3:17–3:18 **Piece of Cake** **[Unit 5]**
I need to pick up a few things
on the way back to school.
Feel like stopping at a store with me?
I'd like to, but I think I'll pass.
I don't have time today.
It's already nearly a quarter to three.

(CHORUS)
Don't worry. We'll be fine.
How long can it take?
It's easy. It'll be a piece of cake.

I need a tube of toothpaste and
a bar of Luvly soap,
some sunscreen, and a bottle of shampoo.
Where would I find makeup?
How about a comb?
Have a look in aisle one or two.

(CHORUS)

I have an appointment
for a haircut at The Spa.
On second thought, they're always
running late.
My class starts in an hour.
I'll never make it now.
How long do you think we'll have to wait?

(CHORUS)

They say there's someone waiting
for a trim ahead of me.
Can I get you some coffee or some tea?
OK. In the meantime,
I'll be getting something strong
for this headache at the pharmacy!

(CHORUS)

▶ 3:37–3:38 **A Perfect Dish**   [Unit 6]

I used to eat a lot of fatty foods,
but now I just avoid them.
I used to like chocolate and lots of sweets,
but now those days are gone.
To tell you the truth,
it was too much trouble.
They say you only live once,
but I'm not crazy about feeling sick.
What was going wrong?
Now I know I couldn't live without this.
Everything's ready.
Why don't you sit down?

(CHORUS)
It looks terrific,
but it smells pretty awful.
What in the world can it be?
It smells like chicken,
and it tastes like fish—
a terrific dish
for you and me—
a perfect dish for you
and me.

I used to be a big meat eater,
now I'm vegetarian,
and I'm not much of a coffee drinker.
I can't stand it anymore.
I'm avoiding desserts with sugar.
I'm trying to lose some weight.
Some things just don't agree with me.
They're bad for me, I'm sure.
Would you like some?
Help yourself.
Isn't it so good for you health?

(CHORUS)

Aren't you going to have some?
Don't you like it?
Wasn't it delicious?
Don't you want some more?

(CHORUS)

▶ 4:13–4:14 **The Colors of Love**   [Unit 7]

Are you sick and tired of working hard day
and night?
Do you like to look at the world in shades of
black and white?
Your life can still be everything that you were
dreaming of.
Just take a look around you and see all the
colors of love.
You wake up every morning and go through
the same old grind.
You don't know how the light at the window
could be so unkind. If blue is the color that
you choose when the road is rough, you know
you really need to believe in the colors of love.

(CHORUS)
The colors of love
are as beautiful as a rainbow.

The colors of love
shine on everyone in the world.
Are negative thoughts and emotions painful
to express?
They're just tiny drops in the ocean of
happiness.
And these are the feelings you must learn to
rise above.
Your whole life is a picture you paint with the
colors of love.

(CHORUS)

▶ 4:28–4:29 **To Each His Own**   [Unit 8]

He doesn't care for Dali.
The colors are too bright.
He says that Picasso
got everything just right.
She can't stand the movies
that are filmed in Hollywood.
She likes Almodóvar.
She thinks he's really good.
He's inspired by everything
she thinks is second-rate.
She's moved and fascinated
by the things he loves to hate.
He's crazy about art that only
turns her heart to stone.
I guess that's why they say
to each his own.
He likes pencil drawings.
She prefers photographs.
He takes her to the the art museum,
but she just laughs and laughs.
He loves the Da Vinci
that's hanging by the door.
She prefers the modern art
that's lying on the floor.
"No kidding! You'll love it. Just wait and see.
It's perfect in every way."
She shakes her head. "It's not for me.
It's much too old and gray."
She thinks he has the worst taste
that the world has ever known.
I guess that's why they say
to each his own.
But when it's time to say goodbye,
they both feel so alone.
I guess that's why they say
to each his own.

▶ 5:16–5:17 **Life in Cyberspace**   [Unit 9]

I'm just fooling around.
Am I interrupting you?
Well, I wanted to know—
what are you up to?
I tried to send some photos,
but it's been so long
that I almost don't remember
how to log on.
So I'm thinking about getting a
new computer.
I don't know what kind. I should have done
it sooner.
But I heard the Panatel is as good as
the rest.
Check it out. Check it out.
You should really check it out.

(CHORUS)
Let's face it—that's life.
That's life in cyberspace.

When you download the pictures,
then you open the files.
If your computer's slow,
then it can take a little while.
From the pull-down menu,
you can print them, too.
But don't forget to save
everything you do.
Scroll it up. Scroll it down.
Put your cursor on the bar.
Then click on the icon,
and you'll see my new car!
The car goes as fast
as the one I had before.
Check it out. Check it out.
You should really check it out.

(CHORUS)

Am I talking to myself, or are you still there?
This instant message conversation's
going nowhere.
I could talk to Liz.
She isn't nearly as nice.
It isn't quite as much fun.
I've done it once or twice.
What's the problem?
Come on. Give it a try.
If you don't want to be friends,
at least tell me why.
Did you leave to make a call
or go out to get some cash?
Did the photos I sent make your
computer crash?

(CHORUS)

▶ 5:31–5:32 **What Would You Do?**
[Unit 10]

What would you do
if I got a tattoo with your name?
What would you say
if I dyed my hair for you?
What would you do
if I sang outside your window?
What would you think
if I told you I loved you?

(CHORUS)
I hate to say this,
but I think you're making a big mistake.
By tomorrow,
I'm sure you'll be sorry.

What would you do
if I sent you a love letter?
Would you say it was wrong
and send it back to me?
What would you think
if I pierced my ears? Would you care?
Would you think
that I had lost all my modesty?

(CHORUS)

Well, give it some thought.
I know I could make you happy.
Are you kidding?
You'd have to be nuts to ask me.
It's no mistake. I'm sure
that my heart is yours.
I have to find a way
to make you mine.

(CHORUS)

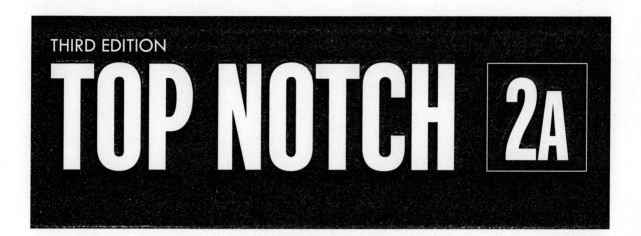

WORKBOOK

JOAN SASLOW
ALLEN ASCHER

with Terra Brockman and Julie C. Rouse

Getting Acquainted

읽히다. 훈계하다.

1 Look at the pictures. Write the correct greeting under each picture. Use words from the box.

| bow | hug | kiss | shake hands |

1. ___bow___   2. ___shake hands___   3. ___kiss___   4. ___hug___

2 Complete the conversation. Write the letter on the line.

A: You look familiar. Haven't we met before?

B: _d_
   1.

A: Aren't you from Canada?

B: _e_
   2.

A: I know! I think we met at Joan's house last month.

B: _a_
   3.

A: Yes, that's right. What have you been up to?

B: _c_
   4.

A: Well, it was nice to see you again.

B: _b_
   5.

A: That would be great. Here's my card.

a. Of course! You work with Joan.

b. You, too. We should keep in touch.

c. Not much. Actually, I'm on my way to a class.

d. I don't think so. I'm not from around here.

e. Yes, I am. I'm from Vancouver.

3 Read the conversation in Exercise 2 again. Circle the subjects the people talk about.

family   religion   (job)   age   weather   nationality

4 When you meet someone new, what subjects do you talk about? Write a ✔ next to the topics you usually talk about. Write an ✗ next to the topics you don't like to talk about.

__✔__ 1. my family   ___ 4. my age   __✗__ 7. politics

___ 2. my religion   __✔__ 5. my hometown or country   __✔__ 8. my job

__✔__ 3. the weather   ___ 6. sports   ___ 9. other: _____

5 Complete each sentence with the present perfect. Use contractions when possible.

1. A: _Do you have_ any coffee today?
   <u>you / have</u>

   B: Yes, _I have_ two cups.
   <u>I / have</u>

2. A: _____ to Europe?
   <u>you / be</u>

   B: Yes, _____ to Spain.
   <u>we / be</u>

3. A: _____ this week?
   <u>you / exercise</u>

   B: Yes, _____ to the gym twice.
   <u>I / go</u>

4. A: _____ any books lately?
   <u>you / read</u>

   B: No, _____ too busy.
   <u>I / be</u>

6 Complete the questions with the correct form of the verbs from the box.
Use each verb only once. Then write your own responses. When you answer <u>yes</u>,
add specific information, using the simple past tense.

be	check	eat	meet	~~see~~

1. "Have you _seen_ any good movies lately?"

   (YOU) _Yes, I have. I saw Toy Story 3 last week._

2. "Have you _____ any famous people?"

   (YOU) _____

3. "Have you _____ to Europe?"

   (YOU) _____

4. "Have you _____ lunch today?"

   (YOU) _____

5. "Have you _____ your e-mail today?"

   (YOU) _____

7 Complete the conversation with the present perfect or the simple past tense.
Use contractions when possible.

Joe: _____ this tour before? I hear it's great.
     <u>1. you / take</u>

Trish: Yes, I have. I _____ to Russia with this group two years ago.
       <u>2. come</u>

       It _____ a wonderful trip. _____ here before?
          <u>3. be</u>   <u>4. you / be</u>

Joe: Yes, I _____ Moscow in 2012, but I _____ much of the city.
           <u>5. visit</u>   <u>6. not / see</u>

     It _____ a business trip. I'm really excited about *this* trip!
        <u>7. be</u>

Trish: Me too. I _____ the brochures several times last night. I can't wait to see all
              <u>8. read</u>

       these places again. By the way, _____ Peter, our tour guide?
                                        <u>9. you / meet</u>

Joe: No, but I'd like to.

Trish: Come. I'll introduce you.

8 Complete the sentences. Circle the correct words.

1. Have you visited the Louvre (yet / ever)?

2. I haven't been to the opera (already / yet).

3. Who is she? I haven't (ever / before) seen her.

4. Has Evan (yet / ever) tried ceviche (already / before)?

5. We've only been here one day, but we've (already / yet) taken a lot of pictures.

6. My parents have been to Italy (ever / before).

7. Has she (yet / ever) gone sightseeing in New York?

8. Have they (already / before) seen the new Brad Pitt movie?

9 Complete the conversations. Write questions or answers in the present perfect. Use <u>already</u>, <u>yet</u>, <u>ever</u>, or <u>before</u>.

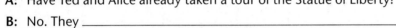

1. **A:** _____?

   B: Yes, he has. George went horseback riding last summer.

2. **A:** Have Ted and Alice already taken a tour of the Statue of Liberty?

   B: No. They _____.

3. **A:** _____?

   B: Yes. I've been to London several times.

4. **A:** _____?

   B: No, but they plan to go to the top of Willis Tower tomorrow.

5. **A:** Has Lisa ever tried Turkish coffee?

   B: Yes. She _____.

10 Look at Anne Marie and Gilbert's to-do list for their vacation in Toronto. Anne Marie has checked what they have already done.

✓ – take a tour of the university

✓ – meet Michel for dinner on Spadina Avenue

– visit the Bata Shoe Museum

✓ – see a musical downtown

– take a boat trip around Toronto Harbor

✓ – go shopping at the Eaton Centre

Now finish Anne Marie's postcard to her friend. Write what she and Gilbert have already done and what they haven't done yet. Use the present perfect.

Dear Agnes,   Sunday, August 6

Gilbert and I are having a wonderful time in Toronto.

We've done so many things! _____

_____

_____

_____

_____

_____

_____

See you when we get back.

Love,

Anne Marie

LESSON 3

EXTRA READING COMPREHENSION

11 Read the article on page 8 in the Student's Book again. Answer the questions.

1. What is non-verbal communication? _____

2. What kind of handshakes do North Americans expect? _____

3. On how many hands do Chinese indicate the numbers one to ten? _____

4. What gesture means "good-bye" in southern Europe? _____

5. What advice does the article give? _____

12 Read the information about greetings in Asia. Then read the statements and check true, false, or no information.

GETTING GREETINGS RIGHT

The traditional greeting in Asia is a bow. In fact, there are different types of bows used in greetings throughout Asia. For example, in Japan, China, and Korea, people bow, but in Japan the bow is usually lower. In India and nearby countries in South Asia, most people put their hands together and bow just a little.

While each Asian culture has its own traditional special greeting, these days, don't be surprised if people in Asia just shake your hand.

	true	false	no information
1. People in China, Japan, and Korea bow when they greet someone.	☐	☐	☐
2. In Korea, people usually bow lower than in Japan.	☐	☐	☐
3. In India, you shouldn't touch the person you are greeting.	☐	☐	☐
4. People in many places in South Asia use a similar greeting.	☐	☐	☐

13 **Complete the sentences about yourself.**

1. In this country, the most common greeting is _____.

2. When I greet someone for the first time, I usually _____.

3. When I greet a family member or close friend, I usually _____.

FACTOID

History of the Handshake
Shaking hands was a way of making sure that people were not carrying a weapon such as a knife or sword. When you shook hands, you were saying, "Look, I don't have a weapon. I trust you. Let's be friends."

LESSON 4

14 **Complete the chart. Write things you've done and things you haven't done but would like to do.**

	Things I've done	Things I'd like to do
climb	climb Mt. Kilimanjaro	climb Mt. Everest

	Things I've done	Things I'd like to do
climb		
visit		
go sightseeing in		
learn		
go to the top of		
see		
try		
meet		
take a tour of		

15 **CHALLENGE.** Look at your experiences in Exercise 14. Write about three things you've done using already or before. Describe each experience with a participial adjective.

> *I've already climbed Mt. Kilimanjaro in Tanzania. It was thrilling!*

1. _____
2. _____
3. _____

Now write about three things you haven't done but would like to do. Use yet, have never, or haven't ever.

1. _____
2. _____
3. _____

GRAMMAR BOOSTER

A Look at the answers. Write information questions, using the question words in parentheses.

1. **A:** (Where) _____?
   B: He's lived in Santiago, Budapest, and Kyoto.

2. **A:** (How) _____?
   B: It's been great—sunny and warm every day!

3. **A:** (What) _____?
   B: Sophie has studied English, Spanish, and Japanese.

4. **A:** (Which) _____?
   B: They've gone to the Metropolitan Museum of Art and the Museum of Modern Art.

5. **A:** (How many) _____?
   B: She's been to Paris three times.

6. **A:** (Who) _____?
   B: I've met Mr. Russ, Mr. Sherman, and Ms. Savidge.

B Rewrite each sentence, changing the placement of yet or already.

1. We've taken that tour already. _____
2. They haven't yet climbed Mt. McKinley. _____
3. Has he eaten dinner already? _____
4. I've already gone sightseeing in Prague. _____
5. She hasn't tried Vietnamese food yet. _____

C Complete the sentences. Circle the correct words.

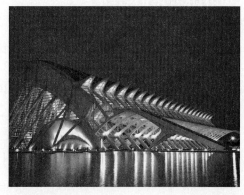

City of Arts and Sciences—Valencia, Spain

1. Have you (yet / already) taken pictures of the City of Arts and Sciences building?

2. Josefina hasn't had her lunch (yet / already).

3. Ryan has finished college (yet / already).

4. Has Michelle (ever / before) been to Greece?

5. My parents have (ever / never) gone on a cruise.

6. I haven't (ever / never) studied Italian.

7. Ruth has (ever / never) tried duck before.

8. Simone is from Paris, but she's never gone to the top of the Eiffel Tower (ever / before)!

D Think of a frightening, a thrilling, a fascinating, and a disgusting experience. Write questions with <u>ever</u>.

> 1. frightening: *Have you ever jumped out of an airplane?*

1. frightening: _____

2. thrilling: _____

3. fascinating: _____

4. disgusting: _____

Now write short answers to your questions.

1. _____   3. _____

2. _____   4. _____

E **CHALLENGE.** What are four things that you've never done? Write sentences using the words in parentheses.

1. (never) _____

2. (not ever) _____

3. (never, before) _____

4. (never, ever) _____

A Read the run-on sentences. Write each sentence correctly. Separate the independent clauses with a period or combine them with a coordinating conjunction, such as <u>and</u> or <u>but</u>.

1. My parents went on a cruise to the Bahamas they haven't been to Bermuda yet.

   _____

   _____

2. I've been to the top of the CN Tower, the view is amazing.

   _____

   _____

3. They went skiing in the Himalayas, the trip was thrilling.

   _____

   _____

4. I've tried snails before they were disgusting.

   _____

   _____

5. Devin has never traveled to continental Europe he has visited Ireland before.

   _____

   _____

6. We have met before we were on the same sightseeing tour yesterday.

   _____

   _____

7. He's from Russia, he has studied English, he would like to learn Mandarin.

   _____

   _____

B Look at Exercise C on page 11 in the Student's Book. On a separate sheet of paper, write your partner's experience. Describe what happened, where your partner was, who your partner was with, and how he or she felt.

C After you write about your partner's experience in Exercise B, check to see if you have written any run-on sentences. Be sure to use a period to separate the independent clauses or use connecting words to combine them.

UNIT 2 Going to the Movies

1 Complete the sentences with words or expressions from the box.

a bunch of	Frankly	I can't stand	It's my treat	I've heard

1. There are _____ good new comedies on Netclips. I can't decide which one to watch.
2. _____ the new Leonardo DiCaprio movie is fantastic. Have you seen it yet?
3. I have two tickets for the 10:00 show. Would you like to go? _____.
4. *The Wolf of Wall Street?* _____, I'm too tired for a three-hour epic!
5. _____ horror movies. I watch movies to relax—not to be frightened.

2 Answer the questions about your own movie preferences.

1. What actor or actress are you a big fan of? _____
2. What movie genres are you usually in the mood for? _____
3. What was the last movie you saw in a theater? _____
4. What was the last movie you watched at home? _____

LESSON 1

3 Complete the posting from an online movie message board. Use <u>since</u> or <u>for</u>.

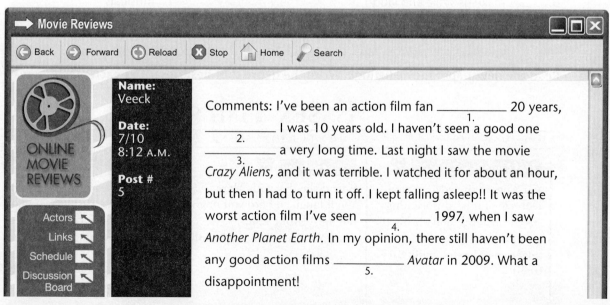

Movie Reviews

Back Forward Reload Stop Home Search

ONLINE MOVIE REVIEWS

Actors
Links
Schedule
Discussion Board

Name: Veeck

Date: 7/10 8:12 A.M.

Post # 5

Comments: I've been an action film fan _____ 20 years,
1.
_____ I was 10 years old. I haven't seen a good one
2.
_____ a very long time. Last night I saw the movie
3.
Crazy Aliens, and it was terrible. I watched it for about an hour,
but then I had to turn it off. I kept falling asleep!! It was the
worst action film I've seen _____ 1997, when I saw
4.
Another Planet Earth. In my opinion, there still haven't been
any good action films _____ *Avatar* in 2009. What a
5.
disappointment!

4 Look at the pictures. Then complete the conversation.

Patty: Hi, Rosemary. Sorry I'm late. Have you been here long?

Rosemary: For about twenty minutes. What happened?

Patty: First _____. I ran to catch it, but it pulled away. And
1.
_____ because it was raining. So, I went back home to get my car.
2.
Then _____. Finally I got here, but _____.
3. 4.
It took me about ten minutes before I found one!

Rosemary: Well, you're here now. Let's go see the movie!

5 Match each movie genre with the correct description. Write the letter on the line.

1. _____ feature fast-paced, exciting, and dangerous situations
2. _____ are drawn by hand or created on a computer
3. _____ tell a story with singing and dancing
4. _____ give us information about real people and things
5. _____ usually take place in the future
6. _____ make us smile and laugh
7. _____ focus on characters' problems and emotions

a. dramas
b. documentaries
c. science-fiction films
d. action films
e. animated films
f. musicals
g. comedies

6 Read the newspaper movie listings. Write the genre that best describes each movie.

ESSEX TIMES

Friday, May 22   ENTERTAINMENT   page 39

The Fearless Fighter 🎥
You'll be on the edge of your seat. Don't miss this exciting adventure! But don't bring the kids—a little too violent.
Edgewood Theater: 6:00, 8:15, 10:30

Myra's Day 🎥
Spend the day with Myra. You'll laugh so hard you might fall out of your seat!
Plaza Cinema: 4:00, 6:00, 8:00

Goodnight, Mariana 🎥
Mariana tries to find her long lost mother. Her search takes her all over the country. Very sad and touching. Based on a true story.
Castle Theater: 4:00, 6:15, 8:30

Genre: _____   Genre: _____   Genre: _____

7 **CHALLENGE.** Which of the movies from the listing in Exercise 6 would you rather see? Explain your answer.

8 Look at Tom's favorite things and <u>least</u> favorite things. Then read each statement and check <u>true</u> or <u>false</u>, based on Tom's lists.

Tom's Favorite Things

1. comedies
2. a trip to the beach
3. pop music
4. going to the gym
5. rice

Tom's <u>Least</u> Favorite Things

1. documentaries
2. a trip to the mountains
3. classical music
4. going shopping
5. pasta

	true	false
1. Tom would rather see a comedy than a documentary.	☐	☐
2. He'd rather take a trip to the mountains than to the beach.	☐	☐
3. He'd rather listen to classical music than pop music.	☐	☐
4. He'd rather go to the gym than go shopping.	☐	☐
5. Tom would rather eat rice than pasta.	☐	☐

9 Look at the statements in Exercise 8. Write five true statements about your own preferences. Use <u>would rather</u>.

10 Read the online movie reviews. Then complete the chart. Write the genre and choose two adjectives from the box to describe each movie. Circle "thumbs up" if the reviewer recommends the movie or "thumbs down" if he or she doesn't recommend it.

| boring | hilarious | interesting | silly | unforgettable | violent | weird |

THE ALIEN!

I was really looking forward to this: Martians take over a city in the year 2030. I usually love these kinds of movies, but *The Alien!* is just too strange for words. The story doesn't make sense. It was downright stupid!

—Kris Baker

SEARCH FOR THE LOST KINGDOM

This is going to be a blockbuster hit! The acting was terrific! A little too much killing for me, but it was still a great movie. I won't forget this movie for a long time!

—Ajay007

DAD'S BACK!

In *Dad's Back!*, Moran Silva films himself and his real family for a whole month. It sounds boring, but you'll be surprised at how entertaining the movie is. I strongly recommend this film to anyone looking for a good laugh.

—Marty19

DON'T SCREAM NOW

A film about a killer monster is scary and exciting, right? Not this one! It was not interesting at all! Almost everyone gets killed, and still I couldn't stay awake! I'd rather have stayed home and read a book.

—Yasir

Movie title	Genre	Adjectives	Reviewer's opinion	
The Alien!			👍	👎
Search for the Lost Kingdom			👍	👎
Dad's Back!			👍	👎
Don't Scream Now			👍	👎

11 Complete the conversation. Write the letter on the line.

A: Hi, Janelle. Seen any good movies recently?

B: _____
     1.

A: *Play Time*? What kind of movie is that?

B: _____
     2.

A: Well, what is it about?

B: _____
     3.

A: That doesn't sound very funny. Was it any good?

B: _____
     4.

A: The funniest? Wow! Who was in it?

B: _____
     5.

A: So you think I would like it?

B: _____
     6.

a. It was terrific. It might be the funniest film I've seen this year.

b. It's a comedy.

c. Definitely. I highly recommend it.

d. Yeah, I just saw *Play Time* at the Art Cinema.

e. It's about some high school kids who don't want to graduate.

f. It stars Wilson Grant—he was really hilarious.

12 **CHALLENGE.** Write your own review about a movie you've seen. Use the reviews in Exercise 10 for support. In your review, answer the following questions: What kind of movie was it? Who was in it? What was it about? Was it funny? Romantic? Thought-provoking? Would you recommend it?

LESSON **4**

13 Read the article *Can Violent Movies or TV Programs Harm Children?* on page 22 in the Student's Book again. Then read each statement and check <u>true</u> or <u>false</u>, according to the information in the article.

EXTRA READING
COMPREHENSION

	true	false
1. It's OK for children to watch violence in animated TV shows and movies.	☐	☐
2. Children who watch a lot of fighting and killing on TV are more likely to act violently as adults.	☐	☐
3. Eight is a safe age for children to start watching violent movies and TV shows.	☐	☐
4. Violence is normal, so children should be exposed to it.	☐	☐
5. Children should learn that there are consequences for doing bad things.	☐	☐
6. Parents should watch and discuss violent TV programs with their very young children.	☐	☐

14 Read the online blog post. Then answer the questions.

How can I protect my kids from media violence?

08 APR 2014 10:05 PM

James F.
<u>view profile</u>

The forecast is for rain all weekend, so I thought I'd rent some movies for the kids to watch. When we looked at the movie list on the television, my nine-year-old son clicked on the new release section. Every movie he picked had a gun or an explosion in the picture. My six-year-old wanted a movie based on one of his favorite toys. He begged me to rent it, "Please, Dad. I have the toys. Why can't I see the movie?" But this movie is not for children. According to the reviews I've read, it's very scary and pretty bloody. We decided to rent a popular animated film I found in the family section, but even that had fighting in it. And the violent scenes were also silly and funny. Frankly, I think that's sending kids a bad message.

I was so upset that I decided to do some research on children and media violence. Did you know that between the ages of four and eighteen, the average child sees 200,000 acts of violence on TV and other media— including 40,000 murders? Also, 60 to 90% of the most popular video games have violent subject matter. Another study found that 61% of television programs show some violence, and 43% of these violent scenes are used to make people laugh!

Why can't the entertainment industry make kids' movies and TV shows that are actually appropriate for kids? And when will they stop selling toys based on violent movies and video games that young children should not see or play? Maybe next time it rains, I'll take my kids to the library instead!

1. What is James F.'s nine-year-old son interested in? _____

2. What does his six-year-old want to see? _____

3. What does James F. rent? _____

4. Why is he upset? _____

5. What does he think the entertainment industry should do? _____

_____

6. Do you agree with James F.? Explain your answer. _____

_____

15 Complete the statements, according to the blog post in Exercise 14. Circle the letter.

1. Between the ages of four and eighteen, the average child sees _____ on TV and in other media.
   a. 40,000 television programs   b. 200,000 murders   c. 40,000 murders

2. _____ of all TV shows contain violent scenes.
   a. More than half   b. Half   c. Less than half

3. Violence on TV is often meant to be seen as _____.
   a. unforgettable   b. funny   c. scary

GRAMMAR BOOSTER

A Read the sentence in column A. Then decide if the sentence in column B is <u>true</u> or <u>false</u>.

A	B	true	false
1. She's been living in Milan for two years.	She still lives in Milan.	☐	☐
2. He's lived in Quito since 2011.	He doesn't live in Quito now.	☐	☐
3. I've climbed Mt. Sorak.	I am climbing Mt. Sorak now.	☐	☐
4. How long have you been reading that book?	You are still reading the book.	☐	☐
5. She's written a review of the new movie.	She's finished writing the review.	☐	☐
6. We've been waiting to see *Gravity*.	We've already seen *Gravity*.	☐	☐

B Think of three activities that you enjoy. When did you start? For each activity, write one present perfect sentence and one present perfect continuous sentence. Use <u>for</u> or <u>since</u>.

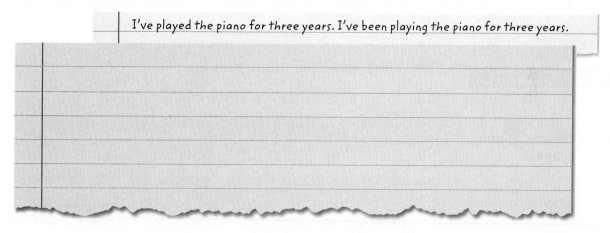

I've played the piano for three years. I've been playing the piano for three years.

C Complete each statement with the present perfect continuous.

1. I _____ really good things about the new Keira Knightley movie.

hear
2. Jimmy _____ me DVDs to watch on the weekends.

give
3. *Ski Trip* _____ terrible reviews.

get
4. *Planet X* _____ a lot of money since it came out last week.

make
5. Audrey's grandparents _____ for her acting classes.

pay
6. Joe and Clem _____ around Europe and Asia for nine months.

travel
7. We _____ for a movie for a half hour. Just choose something!

look

D Complete the sentences. Circle the correct words.

1. I (prefer / would rather) see a silly movie than a violent movie.
2. Annabelle (likes / would rather) classic films.
3. We (prefer / would rather) to order tickets online.
4. She would (like / rather) to watch a romantic comedy.
5. Would you (prefer / rather) sit in the middle or on the aisle?
6. No soda for me. I (prefer / would rather) water.
7. Oscar (prefers / would rather) not go to the movies tonight.

E Look at the answers. Write questions with <u>like</u>, <u>prefer</u>, or <u>would</u> <u>rather</u>.
   There is more than one correct answer.

1. **A:** _____?
   B: A drama. I'm not that big on musicals.

2. **A:** _____?
   B: Popcorn, please. I don't eat candy.

3. **A:** _____?
   B: Definitely a movie. Plays are fine, but I really love movies.

4. **A:** _____?
   B: Saturday works for me. I'm busy on Sunday.

5. **A:** _____?
   B: I'm not in the mood for Chinese food. What about Mexican?

6. **A:** _____?
   B: It doesn't matter to me. You choose.

WRITING BOOSTER

A Write a topic sentence for the following paragraph.

> **Topic sentence:** _____
>
>   People don't imitate the behavior they see in movies. Would you try jumping from the roof of one tall building to another because you saw it in an action film? We live in a violent world. Just open any newspaper—or history book. What happens in real life is more violent than what happens in movies, and violence is not new. Violent entertainment has been around for a long time. Think about the gladiators in ancient Rome.

B Why do some people think violence in movies is harmful? Why do others think it isn't? Complete the chart with people's opinions. Look at Exercise A above and the article on page 22 of the Student's Book for ideas.

Violence in movies	
Harmful	**Not harmful**
Can make children more aggressive	

C On a separate sheet of paper, write two paragraphs of three to five sentences each with details about the following topics. Then write and add a topic sentence for each paragraph.

Paragraph 1

The best movie you ever saw and why you liked it.

Paragraph 2

The worst movie you ever saw and why you couldn't stand it.

Staying in Hotels

1 Look at the hotel bill. Then answer the questions.

```
Mr. Philip Paul                              ROOM      1631
11 Rue Ravignan                           ARRIVAL     09/14        NOVA
Place Emil Goudeau                     DEPARTURE     09/16        HOTEL
75018 Paris, France                          TIME    15:52
CLUB ONE MEMBER # PP2139

DATE    REFERENCE    DESCRIPTION           AMOUNT

9/14    13:13        Local Call            Free (Club One member)
9/14    08:32        Overseas Call         40.34
9/14    3036         Internet access       Free (Club One member)
9/14    2765         Laundry               36.00
9/14                 Room 1631             179.00
9/14    3036         Internet access       Free (Club One member)
9/14    2762         Room Service          18.92
9/15    2762         Room Service          26.45
9/15    09:52        Local Call            Free (Club One member)
9/15    428          Photocopies           Free (Club One member)
9/15    3036         Internet access       Free (Club One member)
9/15    758          Local Fax             Free (Club One member)
9/15                 Room 1631             179.00
9/15    09562        Airport Shuttle       30.00

                     BALANCE               509.71
                     VAT 7.00%             35.68
                     TOTAL INCLUDING VAT   545.39
```

1. What date did Mr. Paul check in? _____

2. How much did he pay for phone calls, faxes, and Internet service? _____

3. How many nights did Mr. Paul stay at the hotel? _____

4. What is the total amount of the hotel bill? _____

2 Check the hotel services that Mr. Paul used at the Nova Hotel, according to the hotel bill.

☐   ☐   ☐   ☐   ☐

☐   ☐   ☐   ☐   ☐

3 Which services are important to these hotel guests? Read what each person says and write the hotel service on the line.

I like to have breakfast in my room before I get dressed for the day.

1. _____

I like to work out for an hour in the gym every day before breakfast.

2. _____

I have a very important meeting in the morning. I can't oversleep!

3. _____

I check e-mail and work on my laptop in the evening.

4. _____

I would rather swim for exercise than lift weights.

5. _____

I don't want to do laundry on my vacation!

6. _____

LESSON 1

4 Put the conversation in order. Write the number on the line.

___1___ Can I speak with Kevin Mercer, please? He's staying in room 376.

_____ That's right.

_____ Yes. Could you tell him Barbara called? Please ask him to call me back at 228-555-3156.

_____ One moment, please . . . I'm sorry. There's no answer. Can I take a message?

_____ Barbara at 228-555-3156?

_____ Is that all?

___7___ Yes, that's it. Thank you very much.

5 The fortune-teller is predicting the future. Read her predictions. Then rewrite the sentences using <u>will</u>.

2. Then, you're taking a trip to Barcelona.

3. When you are in Barcelona, you meet an old friend.

4. Your friend is going to offer you an exciting job in Spain.

1. Next week, you are going to win a prize.

5. Next month, you are moving to Spain.

1. _____

2. _____

3. _____

4. _____

5. _____

6 Rewrite the following future statements and questions using <u>will</u>.

1. I'm going to call her later today. _____

2. She's going to stop at the front desk first. _____

3. My uncle is meeting my father at the airport. _____

4. What time does the tour group get back? _____

5. When are they going to make a reservation? _____

6. Where is your grandmother staying in Madrid? _____

7 Read the phone conversation. Then complete the message sheet.

A: Hello. I'd like to speak with Ms. Marina Santiago, please.

B: One moment, please. I'll ring Ms. Santiago's room . . .
I'm sorry, but there's no answer. Would you like to
call back later?

A: No, I'd like to leave a message. Please tell her that
Anna Streed called. I'll be at 664-555-8723 until 5:00 today.

B: OK, Ms. Anna Street . . .

A: No, it's Streed, S-T-R-E-E-D—that's "D" as in "door."

B: OK, Ms. Streed. I'll make sure she gets the message.

To _Marina Santiago_

Date ___9/14___ Time ___3:15___ A.M. ☐ P.M. ☒

WHILE YOU WERE OUT

☐ Mr./ ☐ Ms./ ☐ Mrs. _____

Phone _____
    Area code   Number   Extension

☐ telephoned   ☐ please call
☐ returned your call   ☐ will call back

Message: _____

_____

LESSON **2**

8 Look at the sentences in the box. Write the correct sentence below each picture.

> If you book the hotel early, you will save money.
> If you request rollaway beds, someone will bring them to your room.
> If a guest is in a hurry, a taxi is faster than the shuttle.
> If you book a suite, breakfast is free.

1. _____

2. _____

3. _____

4. _____

9 Write <u>factual</u> if the conditional sentence expresses a fact. Write <u>future</u> if it expresses a future result.

_____ 1. If you check in early, you'll get the room you want.

_____ 2. If a hotel room has wireless Internet, guests don't have to go to a business center to check e-mail.

_____ 3. We will provide wake-up service in the morning if you request it.

_____ 4. If you take something from the minibar, you'll have to pay extra.

10 Find the errors and write the correct sentences.

1. If you will hurry, you'll catch the shuttle. _____

2. If the fitness center is still open, I go swimming. _____

3. If there will not be rental cars at the airport, will you take a bus? _____

4. If I make my reservation early I'll get a cheaper room. _____

W20   UNIT 3

11   **Label the pictures.**

1.
2.
3.
4.
5.

12   **Look at the pictures. Then complete the conversations.**

1. A: Guest services. May I help you?

B: Yes, please. Could you bring up some _____?
1.
I need clean ones.

A: Certainly.

B: And I could use a _____, too. My hair is wet,
2.
and I don't see one in the bathroom.

A: Sure. We'll bring those up right away. Anything else?

B: Oh, yes. I have a lot of dirty clothes. Could someone
please _____?
3.

A: Yes, of course.

B: I think that's all. Thanks!

2. A: Front Desk. May I help you?

B: Yes, I'd like to go for a swim. Is the _____ still open?
4.

A: No, I'm sorry, it closed at 9:00.

B: Oh. Well, maybe a workout. How about the _____?
5.

A: No, it also just closed.

B: Oh, no. Well, I guess I'll have to do some work then.
Is the _____ still open?
6.

A: No, I'm sorry, it closed at 6:30. But you do have high-speed
Internet access in your room.

B: Oh, OK. Thanks.

13 Read the website on page 34 of the Student's Book again. Then read the statements and check <u>true</u>, <u>false</u>, or <u>no information</u>.

EXTRA READING
COMPREHENSION

	true	false	no information
1. The Plaza is the most expensive hotel.	☐	☐	☐
2. Broadway at Times Square Hotel is in the Theater District.	☐	☐	☐
3. Yotel has suites.	☐	☐	☐
4. Hotel Peninsula is a budget hotel.	☐	☐	☐
5. The Gershwin Hotel is several blocks away from the Empire State Building.	☐	☐	☐
6. The Hotel Newton is pet friendly.	☐	☐	☐

14 Read the travel guide about places to stay in Dublin, Ireland.

SLEEPING IN DUBLIN

€€€ Very expensive / €€ Moderately priced / € Budget

The Shelbourne Hotel

€€€   *History, Location*
Built in 1824, the Shelbourne is the most famous hotel in Dublin and a home-away-from-home for generations of politicians, writers, and actors. In fact, in 1922 the Irish Constitution was written in Room 112! Overlooking Saint Stephen's Green public park in the heart of Dublin, the location is perfect for sightseeing and shopping. Even if you don't stay here, you must go for afternoon tea in the elegant Lord Mayor's Lounge.

restaurant, room service, laundry service, business center, Internet service

The Morgan Hotel

€€€   *Style, Nightlife*
If you're crazy about style, the Morgan Hotel is your place. With very modern décor and designer furniture, this chic hotel is a favorite of people who work in fashion and music. The Morgan is located in the trendy Temple Bar district—an area popular with young people and *the* center of nightlife in Dublin. Note: Can be noisy at night.

restaurant, room service, laundry service, business center, Internet service, fitness room

The Aberdeen Lodge

€€   *Atmosphere, Service*
A short train ride from the Dublin city center, in a neighborhood of beautiful old homes and gardens, the Aberdeen Lodge is the perfect place for a quiet and relaxing stay. The friendly staff welcomes guests with tea and cookies and is very helpful with tourist advice. Suites feature working fireplaces. Don't miss breakfast in the lovely dining room overlooking the garden. Note: There is no elevator.

restaurant, room service, laundry service

The Camden Court

€€   *Convenience, Location*
The Camden Court is a large hotel that offers business travelers a good night's sleep and lot of amenities at an affordable price. Rooms are small but clean and comfortable. A short walk from Saint Stephen's Green, the location is perfect— close to tourist attractions, restaurants, and shopping. The Camden Court is a good choice for business or pleasure.

pool, sauna, fitness room, room service, business center, free Internet service, beauty salon, restaurant, free parking

Trinity College

€   *Price, Location*
Experience student life—without the exams!—at this beautiful, historic university located in the center of Dublin. From June to September, visitors can reserve single and double rooms while students are away for the summer holiday. Rooms are large and clean, but don't expect many amenities or services. Not all rooms have their own bathrooms.

cafeteria-style restaurant, free breakfast

15 Complete the chart. Use the travel guide in Exercise 14 to list an advantage and a disadvantage of each hotel.

Hotel	Advantage	Disadvantage
The Shelbourne Hotel		
The Morgan Hotel		
The Aberdeen Lodge		
The Camden Court		
Trinity College		

16 Read about the people's hotel needs and preferences. Use the travel guide in Exercise 14 to decide the best hotel for each person. Write statements with *If* and *will /won't*.

I want to meet other people my age and walk to clubs at night.

1. _____
_____

Peter broke his leg, but we can't change our flight. We need to be close to the sights and comfortable.

2. _____
_____

I'm traveling in the summer. Location is important to me, but I'm on a budget.

3. _____
_____

I'm attending a conference in Dublin. I'll have to wake up early, so I'd like someplace quiet. Oh, and I've got to be able to exercise.

4. _____
_____

GRAMMAR BOOSTER

A Write sentences. Use <u>have to</u>, <u>must not</u>, <u>don't have to</u>, or <u>doesn't have to</u>.

1. Employees and guests / smoke in the hotel _____

2. Hotel guests / check out before noon _____

3. A guest / use anything from the minibar _____

4. Housekeeping staff / make up the rooms _____

5. Hotel guests / reuse their towels, but they can _____

6. We / forget to unplug the iron _____

B Read the situation. Write a suggestion. Use <u>could</u>, <u>should</u>, <u>ought to</u>, <u>shouldn't</u>, <u>had better</u>, or <u>had better not</u>.

1. The 7:00 show is sold out. _____

2. We have a lot of luggage. _____

3. It's expensive to take a taxi to the airport. _____

4. The play starts at 8:00. _____

5. The Peninsula Hotel is very expensive. _____

6. We don't know where to go for dinner. _____

C Write a rule for each place. Use <u>be supposed to</u> or <u>not supposed to</u>.

1. a hospital: _____ *You're not supposed to use your cell phone in a hospital.* _____

2. a restaurant: _____

3. a movie theater: _____

4. an airplane: _____

5. a museum: _____

6. the library: _____

D Complete the conversation using <u>will</u> or <u>won't</u>. Use contractions when possible.

A: _____ you be staying with us
       1.
    another night?

B: No, we _____. But I think we
             2.
    _____ be back next month.
       3.

A: Great. How _____ you be paying today?
                 4.

B: I _____ use my credit card, if that's OK.
      5.

A: Sure. That _____ be fine.
           6.

E Look at the pictures. What do you think the man is going to do?
Write sentences with a form of <u>be going to</u> or <u>not be going to</u>.

1. _____

2. _____

3. _____

4. _____

5. _____

F Complete the conversations. Use the correct form of <u>be going to</u> if there is a plan
for the future or <u>will</u> if there is not a plan.

1. **A:** Have you decided about your vacation yet?

   B: Yes, we have. We _____ to India!

1. go

   A: Wow! When _____ you _____ ?

2. leave

   B: We _____ out on the 20th.

3. fly

   A: That's fantastic. Where _____ you _____?

4. stay

   B: I don't know yet. I guess we should make hotel reservations—or maybe

   we _____ just _____ something when we arrive.

5. find

2. **A:** Guess what? I _____ into a new apartment next week.

6. move

   B: That's great news! I _____ you if you like. What day _____

7. help

   you _____?

8. move

   A: Thanks! It's this Saturday at 9 A.M. OK?

   B: Oh, no! I _____ my sister at the airport then.

9. pick up

   A: No problem. Just come by when you're free.

A Read the hotel reviews in Exercise 14 on page 22 again. Complete each statement with a reason, according to the information in the reviews. Write the letter on the line.

1. _____ I prefer the Shelbourne . . .

2. _____ I'm going to stay at the Morgan . . .

3. _____ I'd like to stay at the Aberdeen Lodge . . .

4. _____ I'd rather stay at the Camden Court . . .

5. _____ I chose Trinity College . . .

a. because I'm not that big on noisy cities.

b. since I'm looking for the cheapest accommodations.

c. because I'm interested in Irish history.

d. since I want to be in Temple Bar.

e. since I'm going to rent a car.

B Rewrite the sentences in Exercise A, placing the dependent clause at the beginning of each sentence. Use a comma.

1. _____

2. _____

3. _____

4. _____

5. _____

C Look at the hotel reviews in Exercise 14. Which hotel would you rather stay at? Write the name of the hotel in the circle. List reasons with <u>because</u> or <u>since</u> in the boxes.

because

since

because

since

D On a separate sheet of paper, write a paragraph about the hotel you chose in Exercise C. Explain why you would like to stay there. Give reasons, using <u>because</u> or <u>since</u>. Are there any disadvantages? After you write your paragraph, check carefully to make sure that there are no sentence fragments.

1 Complete each sentence with a bad driving habit from the box. Use the -ing form
of each verb.

speed	tailgate	talk on the phone	text	not signal

1. The car behind me is too close! I can see the driver's lipstick color. She's _____!

2. That person is laughing and _____. He's having a conversation while he's driving!

3. That woman is turning right, but she's _____. That's so dangerous!

4. The guy next to me has no hands on the wheel, and he's looking down! I know he's
   _____!

5. He's going 70 miles per hour near a school! He's _____. I'm calling the police!

2 Read the conversations. Complete the missing text in the speech bubbles with the
expressions from the box.

Long time no see.	Congratulations!	I can't complain.	catch up on old times

3   **Choose the correct response. Circle the letter.**

1. "This car was trying to park, and he hit another car. The driver was talking on the phone."
    a. You've got to be kidding!   **b.** Just a moment.   **c.** That's right.

2. "I don't think anyone was hurt in the accident."
    a. I can't complain.   **b.** You're all set.   **c.** Thank goodness for that.

3. "So many people drive and text at the same time."
    a. Congratulations!   **b.** You can say that again.   **c.** Either way.

4. "I just got a new car!"
    a. Here you go.   **b.** Congratulations!   **c.** I can't complain.

4   **Label the car parts.**

1. d a s h b o a r d
2. _ _ _ _ _ _ _ _ _ _ _ _ _
3. _ _ _ _ _ _ _ _ _ _ _ _ _ _
4. _ _ _ _ _

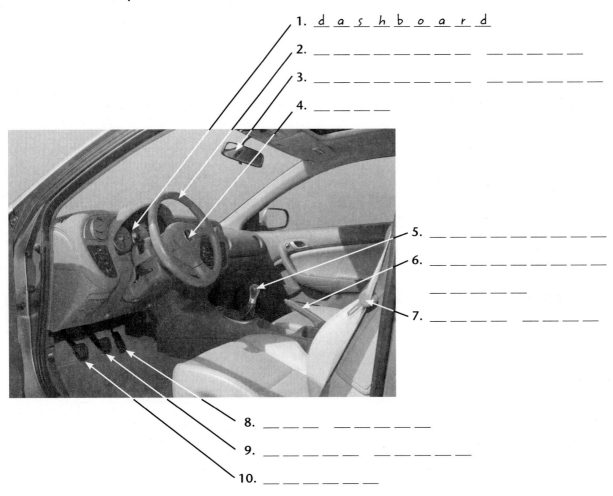

5. _ _ _ _ _ _ _ _ _ _
6. _ _ _ _ _ _ _ _ _
   _ _ _ _ _
7. _ _ _ _ _ _ _ _ _

8. _ _ _ _ _ _ _ _ _
9. _ _ _ _ _ _ _ _ _ _ _
10. _ _ _ _ _ _ _

5 Complete the conversation with the past continuous or the simple past tense.

A: Hi, Sandra. What's wrong?

B: I _____ an accident on the way home today.
   _____1. have_____

A: Oh, no! How _____ it _____?
                                              _____2. happen_____

B: Well, I _____ home when my sister
              ____3. drive____
   _____. She _____
   ___4. call___   ___5. ask___
   what I _____, and I _____
              ___6. do___   ___7. tell___
   her I _____ home and would see
            ____8. go____
   her soon. But she _____ she had a funny
                          ____9. say____
   story that she just <u>had</u> to tell me. Anyway, by the end of the
   story, I _____ so hard I couldn't see—and
               ___10. laugh___
   I _____ right into a stop sign.
      ___11. drive___

6 Choose the correct response. Write the letter on the line.

1. "I had an accident today." _____

2. "Are you OK?" _____

3. "How did it happen?" _____

4. "Luckily, I was wearing my seat belt." _____

5. "Was there much damage?" _____

a. The other driver was speeding.

b. Not really. The other driver will have to replace a taillight.

c. Thank goodness.

d. Yes, I'm fine. No one was hurt.

e. How awful.

7 **CHALLENGE.** Have you or has someone you know ever had an accident? What happened? Write a note to a friend about it.

8 Look at the pictures. Write the letter of the correct picture after each phrasal verb.

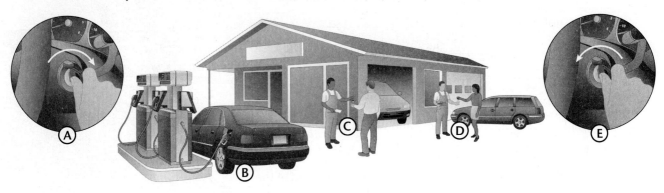

1. fill up _____ 2. turn on _____ 3. drop off _____ 4. turn off _____ 5. pick up _____

9 **CHALLENGE.** Complete the note below. Use the correct phrasal verb from Exercise 8. Sometimes you will need to use direct object pronouns.

> Hi, Lisa!
>
> I made an appointment to have Stan fix the car today. Can you _____
> at the service station this afternoon? Tell Stan that the left turn signal isn't working. ^1.^
> This morning I could _____, but now it's stuck, and I can't seem to ^2.^
> _____ . Ask him to call me when the car is done. I'll _____ ^3.^ ^4.^
> on my way home from work.
>
> Love, Daniel
>
> P.S. While you're there, could you _____ the tank? See you tonight! ^5.^

10 Choose the correct response. Circle the letter.

1. "I'm dropping off my rental car."
   a. It's all ready to go. b. Was everything OK? c. Was there much damage?

2. "Any problems?"
   a. I just filled it up. b. The sunroof won't open. c. I'm sorry to hear that.

3. "What's wrong with the air conditioning?"
   a. It won't close. b. It's out of gas. c. It's making a funny sound.

4. "Is the gas tank full?"
   a. No. That's it. b. Oh, no! I forgot to fill it up. c. I wasn't paying attention.

11 Complete each sentence with a car type from the box.

| a convertible | a minivan | an SUV | a luxury car | a compact car |

1. Mavis loves hiking. She has _____ with four-wheel drive that she can drive on rough roads when she takes a trip to the mountains.

2. If you just need a car that's small and easy to park, _____ would be great for you.

3. Mrs. Jeter drives _____ to take her husband to work and their five children to school every morning.

4. Peter thinks that owning _____ is really cool. He said, "You can have the roof down and enjoy the sun, wind, and beautiful sky when the weather is nice."

5. Jack is the president of a big company, and he drives _____ with expensive leather seats.

12 Read the phone conversation. Then complete the rental form.

Agent: Good afternoon. L & M Car Rental. How can I help you?

Renter: Hello. I'd like to make a reservation for June 10th.

Agent: Certainly. What type of car do you need?

Renter: A compact car.

Agent: Let's see . . . I'm afraid I don't have a compact available for that date. Is a full-size sedan OK?

Renter: That's fine.

Agent: How long do you need the car for?

Renter: For eight days. Can I pick up the car here in Middletown and return it at Bradley Airport?

Agent: Yes, that's fine. But there is a drop-off fee for one-way rentals.

Renter: All right. One last question. Where are you located?

Agent: We're at 355 South Street in Middletown.

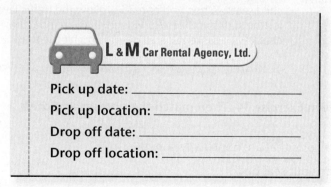

L & M Car Rental Agency, Ltd.

Pick up date: _____
Pick up location: _____
Drop off date: _____
Drop off location: _____

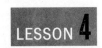

13 Read *Six Tips For Defensive Driving* on page 46 of the Student's Book again. Then read the statements and write <u>D</u> for defensive driving, <u>A</u> for aggressive driving, or <u>I</u> for inattentive driving.

EXTRA READING
COMPREHENSION

1. _____ tailgating to make others go faster

2. _____ following the "3-second rule"

3. _____ multitasking while driving

4. _____ checking your mirrors frequently

5. _____ slowing down in bad weather

6. _____ pulling over to avoid a bad driver

7. _____ cutting other drivers off

8. _____ talking on the phone while driving

14 Read the article about renting a car in the U.S.

Driving in the U.S.A.

Planning a trip to the U.S.? Have you thought about how you'll get around? If you're going to stay in a big city such as New York, Chicago, or San Francisco, public transportation is the most convenient option. However, to travel almost anywhere else in the U.S., you'll need a car.

Car Rental Tips

Requirements: Most car rental agencies require drivers to be at least 25 years old. Some allow younger drivers, but may charge a higher rate. To rent a car in the U.S., you will need a credit card and driver's license. Visitors can usually rent a car and drive with a driver's license from their home country. However, if your license is in a language that doesn't use the Roman alphabet, you should obtain an International Driving Permit in English.

Cost: Car rental rates change often, and you can usually save money by shopping around for the best price. Be sure to check travel and rental agency websites for special sales and discounts. Look for package deals that offer car rental and airfare or hotel for one low price. If your schedule is flexible, compare prices for different travel dates. It is often cheaper to rent a car on weekends or for a full week rather than a few days.

Hidden charges: Always read the small print on your car rental agreement carefully—to check for hidden charges such as taxes, airport surcharges, and drop-off fees (an extra charge for returning a car to a different location from where you picked up). Make sure that you drop off the car with a full tank of gas. Rental agencies charge a fill-up fee and high gas prices if they have to fill up the gas tank.

Safety: Before you leave the car rental lot, inspect the car carefully for damage and make sure everything is working properly. Ask the agent to note any problems on the rental form. Take a few minutes to become familiar with the car. Adjust your seat and mirrors. Locate the controls for the lights, turn signals, and windshield wipers. Then, buckle up! Wear your seat belt, and ask your passengers to wear theirs, too. Most states have seat belt laws, and all states require that young children and babies sit in the back seat in special child seats. When you're ready, follow the traffic laws for the states you'll be driving in. If you're not sure, check with car rental staff before you hit the road.

Find and circle the phrases in the article in Exercise 14. Then match the phrases and their meanings. Write the letter on the line.

1. _____ get around

2. _____ package deals

3. _____ hidden charges

4. _____ fill-up fee

5. _____ buckle up

6. _____ hit the road

a. extra costs that are not clearly stated

b. fasten your seat belt

c. travel from place to place

d. begin a car trip

e. specials that offer two or more services for one price

f. an extra charge for returning a car without a full tank of gas

15 Answer the questions about renting a car in the U.S. Use information from the article in Exercise 14. Explain your answers.

1. I am 23 years old. Can I rent a car? _____

_____

2. Do I need an International Driving Permit to drive in the U.S.? _____

_____

3. Where can I get the best price for a car rental? _____

_____

4. I want to pick up a car in New York and drop it off at Los Angeles International Airport. What hidden charges should I check for? _____

_____

5. We are traveling with small children. Are there any special requirements? _____

_____

GRAMMAR BOOSTER

A Complete each sentence in your own way. Use the past continuous or the simple past tense.

1. They were having dinner when _____.

2. While _____ , it started to rain.

3. While Marie was watching TV, her husband _____.

4. When _____ , I was leaving my office.

5. He had an accident while _____.

B **CHALLENGE.** Look at the pictures. On a separate sheet of paper, write a story about what happened using the words and phrases in the boxes.

drive	run in front of	hit
talk on cell phone	stop	hurt
not pay attention		damage

C Put the words in order and write sentences. If a sentence can be written in two ways, write it both ways.

1. dropped / Margo / off / the car

    Margo dropped off the car. OR Margo dropped the car off.

2. up / it / Sam / picked

    _____

3. the tank / filled / I / up

    _____

4. can't / turn / on / Sue / the headlights

    _____

5. turn / off / I / can't / them

    _____

6. like / He'd / it / to / drop / off / at noon

    _____

7. I / to / need / up / it / fill

    _____

8. picked / the car / William / up / has

    _____

    _____

D Label each underlined noun either <u>common</u> or <u>proper</u>. Then rewrite each sentence, replacing the underlined noun with a subject or object pronoun.

1. *common*
    <u>The car door</u> is making a funny sound.

    It is making a funny sound.

2. <u>Mr. Lee</u> rented the convertible.

    _____

3. The mechanic replaced <u>the taillight</u>.

    _____

4. Alex already called <u>Econo-Car</u>.

    _____

5. <u>The Amigo minivan</u> hit the tree.

    _____

6. My sister will drop off <u>the keys</u>.

    _____

7. Mrs. Lane is going to pick up <u>her son</u> at 5:00.

    _____

A   **Insert commas where necessary in the following sentences.**

1.   You need a driver's license and a credit card to rent a car.

2.   The car rental charge included a drop-off fee a fill-up fee and an airport surcharge.

3.   You should shop around for the best price and make a reservation.

4.   Adjust your seat mirrors and the radio.

5.   Locate the controls for the lights and turn signals.

B   **Combine each pair of sentences into one sentence consisting of two independent clauses. Use <u>and</u>.**

1.   The driver wasn't paying attention. He hit the car in front of him.

_____

2.   It's raining. The sunroof won't close.

_____

3.   Lucy has five kids. She drives a minivan.

_____

4.   The GPS isn't working. We're lost.

_____

C   **Complete the statements. Look back at the article in Exercise 14 for ideas. Add commas.**

1.   Many areas of the U.S. don't have good public transportation. Therefore _____

_____.

2.   Car rental rates change frequently. Therefore _____

_____.

3.   To find a good rate, check travel and car rental agency websites. In addition _____

_____.

4.   Return your rental car with a full tank of gas. If you don't, you'll pay double the regular price for gas.
     In addition _____

_____.

5.   Most states have seat belt laws. Therefore _____

_____.

6.   Small children must sit in the back seat. In addition _____

_____.

D   **On a separate sheet of paper, write about your driving or a friend or family member's driving. Include good and bad driving behaviors.**

Personal Care and Appearance

1 **Complete the sentences with salon or fitness services.**

1. Your fingernails look great. Did you get a __ __◯__ __ __ __ __?

2. His hair was getting long, so he made an appointment for a __◯__ __ __ __ __.

3. I have a lot of tension in my shoulders from sitting at the computer. I need a __ __ __◯__ __ __.

4. After my __ __ __ __ __◯, my skin felt smooth and soft.

5. I love taking __◯__ __ classes. I feel so relaxed afterwards.

Now unscramble the circled letters. What's the word? _____

2 **Complete the conversation with questions from the box. Write the letter.**

> a. Do you think I could get a massage, too?
>
> b. Is it customary to leave a tip?
>
> c. How long will I have to wait?
>
> d. Would it be possible to get a facial?
>
> e. Can I charge it to my room?

Client: _____? I don't have an appointment.

1.

Receptionist: You're in luck. A client just canceled his appointment.

Client: Great. ____?

2.

Receptionist: Yes. But you might have to wait a bit.

Client: ____?

3.

Receptionist: Let's see. I have something at 4:00.

Client: That's fine. ____?

4.

Receptionist: Certainly. Just sign here, please. Then I'll show you to the dressing area.

Client: I have one more question. ____?

5.

Receptionist: That's up to you. But most clients give about 10 percent.

3 How often do you get these salon services? Look at each picture and write a sentence.

1. _____

2. _____

3. _____

4. _____

5. _____

LESSON 1

4 Complete the word webs. Write personal care products on the lines.

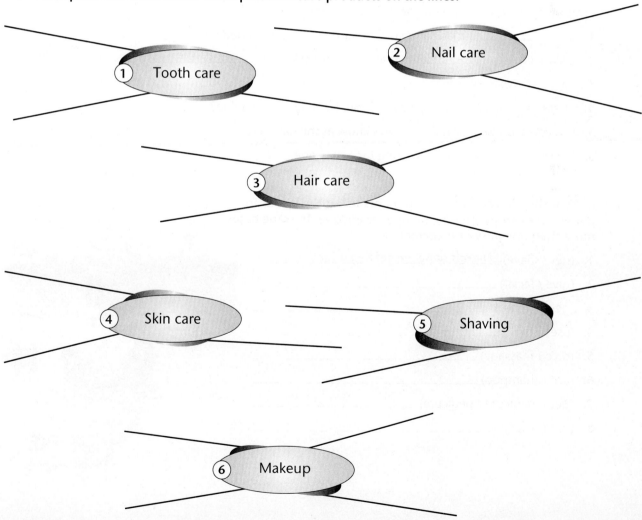

5 Complete the sentences. Circle the correct words.

1. This store doesn't have (much / many) combs.

2. I can't find (some / any) sunscreen, but here's (some / any) body lotion.

3. Do you have (much / a lot of) razors at home?

4. She doesn't have (much / many) hair spray left.

5. Emma needs (some / any) dental floss.

6. Helen doesn't need (some / much) soap.

7. Do you have (any / many) deodorant?

8. I have (some / any) extra shampoo.

9. I found shaving cream, but there aren't (some / any) razors here.

10. Are you out of toothpaste? I have (some / much).

6 Complete each statement or question with <u>someone</u>, <u>no one</u>, or <u>anyone</u>. In some cases, more than one answer is correct.

1. _____ made a ten o'clock appointment for a pedicure.

2. Excuse me. _____ is at the front desk. Can _____ help me?

3. I'm sorry. We don't have _____ available to help you now.

4. There's _____ ahead of you. Do you mind waiting?

5. Did you see _____ you know at the hair salon?

6. There's _____ waiting for a massage.

7 Look at the pictures. Write statements using the words in parentheses and <u>someone</u>, <u>no one</u>, or <u>anyone</u>. In some cases, more than one answer is correct.

1. (get / shave) *There's someone getting a shave.*

2. (give / facial) _____

3. (get / haircut) _____

4. (use / comb) _____

5. (give / massage) _____

6. (use / shampoo) _____

7. (get / manicure / pedicure) _____

8. (use / nail file) _____

LESSON 3

8 Read the article *Cosmetic surgery—for everyone?* on page 56 of the Student's Book again. Then match the terms with their definitions.

EXTRA READING COMPREHENSION

1. _____ chocoholic
2. _____ liposuction
3. _____ hair restoration
4. _____ face-lift
5. _____ chemical peel

a. surgery to correct baldness
b. someone who likes chocolate very much and eats it all the time
c. surgery to remove wrinkles and other signs of aging from the face
d. treatment for wrinkles that removes the top layer of skin on the face
e. surgery to remove fat from the body

9 Read the article about ways to improve personal appearance.

Look Great – Without Cosmetic Surgery

Want to lose weight? Look younger? More and more people are turning to cosmetic surgery. While liposuction or a face-lift might sound like an easy way to get the results you want, it's important to remember that cosmetic surgery is, in fact, surgery. And surgery is not easy. It's expensive, painful, and potentially dangerous. So, before you go under the knife, give these safe, low-cost ways to improve your appearance a try.

1. Get enough sleep. It's called "beauty sleep" for a reason. Nighttime is when your skin and hair cells renew and repair themselves. Also, more blood flows to your skin when you're sleeping, making it brighter. Most people know that lack of sleep can cause dark circles under your eyes. But many don't realize that not getting eight hours of sleep a night can also lead to wrinkles and weight gain.

2. Drink a lot of water. Get into the habit of drinking more water. Well-hydrated skin is less likely to develop blemishes or wrinkles. For clearer, smoother skin, try to drink at least eight glasses of water a day. The more water you drink, the better your skin will look. Also, drinking water throughout the day will curb your appetite—making it easier to eat less and lose weight.

3. Exercise regularly. The physical benefits of exercise include reduced body fat and more toned muscles. While 60 minutes of daily vigorous exercise is ideal, begin with a reasonable goal—maybe 30 minutes three times a week. Choose something you enjoy, and enroll in a class, join a team, or make plans to work out regularly with a group of friends.

4. Eat a healthy diet. To lose weight, you need to change your eating habits. You should choose foods that are low in fat and low in calories. You probably knew that already, but did you know that some foods can also improve the appearance of your skin and hair? For beautiful skin, eat foods rich in antioxidants. Dark-colored fruits and vegetables contain antioxidants, which help repair sun damage and prevent wrinkles. Blueberries, spinach, and carrots have a lot of antioxidants. For shiny, healthy hair, eat foods high in lean protein like fish, beans, and nuts. These foods may also help prevent hair loss.

What's good for your health is also good for your looks. So, get a good night's sleep and some exercise. Drink lots of water and eat fresh, natural foods—mostly fruits and veggies. It costs almost nothing and doesn't hurt, so what have you got to lose? Except maybe a few kilos!

10 Complete the chart. Use information from the article. How much sleep, water, and exercise does the article recommend? What types of foods does it suggest?

	What the article recommends
sleep	
water	
exercise	
diet	

11 What are the results of doing what the article recommends?

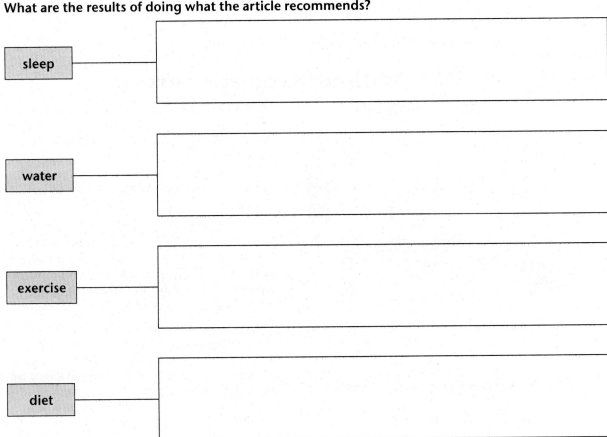

sleep

water

exercise

diet

12 **CHALLENGE.** How much sleep and exercise do you get? How much water do you drink? What types of foods do you eat? After reading the article, what would you like to do differently? Why?

13 Think of a famous person or someone you know that represents both inner and outer beauty. Describe the person's inner qualities on the lines inside the head. Describe the person's physical features on the lines outside the head.

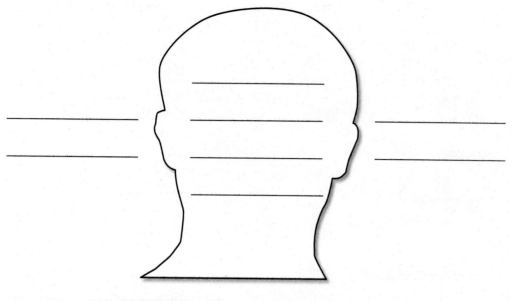

Name of person: _____

14 Complete the statements with words from the box.

attractive	health	heart	inner
kindness	modest	outer	patient

1. Someone who is a good listener and lets others speak is _____.

2. Beautiful skin and hair and a nice body are features of _____ beauty.

3. Goodness, _____ to other people, truthfulness, and happiness with life are qualities of _____ beauty.

4. Someone who has nice physical features is _____.

5. The condition of a person's body is called _____.

6. Someone who doesn't talk proudly about his or her own appearance or abilities is

   _____.

7. "The best and most beautiful things in the world cannot be seen, nor touched . . . but are felt in the

   _____." –Helen Keller

GRAMMAR BOOSTER

A Look in the medicine cabinet. Write sentences about the products you see, using words from the box.

bar	bottle	can	package	tube

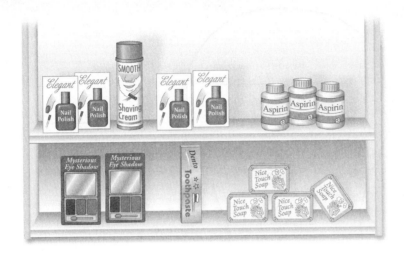

1. _____There are four bottles of nail polish._____

2. _____

3. _____

4. _____

5. _____

6. _____

B Answer the questions about your own personal care products. Write complete sentences with <u>some</u> or <u>any</u>.

1. Do you have any dental floss at home?

   _____

2. Do you need some toothpaste from the store?

   _____

3. Is there any shaving cream in your bathroom?

   _____

4. Are you wearing any perfume or aftershave now?

   _____

5. Do you have some sunscreen at home?

   _____

6. Is there any makeup in your bathroom?

   _____

7. Would you like some hand lotion?

   _____

C Write a ✔ next to the sentences that are correct.

1. ☐ a. There isn't enough soap.
   ☐ b. There isn't too many soap.
2. ☐ a. Do you have too much razors?
   ☐ b. Do you have too many razors?
3. ☐ a. I don't have too many makeup.
   ☐ b. I don't have enough makeup.
4. ☐ a. Does she have too many toothpaste?
   ☐ b. Does she have enough toothpaste?
5. ☐ a. There isn't too much shampoo.
   ☐ b. There isn't too many shampoo.

D Complete each sentence with <u>too much</u>, <u>too many</u>, or <u>enough</u>.

1. I couldn't wash my hair. There wasn't _____ shampoo left.
2. I'm going to the store. Do you have _____ flour to make the cake?
3. There are just _____ people here. I don't feel like waiting.
4. Don't you think that's _____ money for a pedicure? It's too expensive.
5. You bought _____ nail files. We only need one.

E Complete each sentence with <u>fewer</u> or <u>less</u>.

1. Bridget should wear _____ makeup. She looks beautiful without it!
2. Budget hotels have _____ amenities than expensive hotels.
3. This film has _____ violence than that new action adventure movie.
4. The compact car will use _____ gas than the SUV.
5. Which ticket line has _____ people waiting in it?
6. The rental agency has _____ cars with manual transmission than with automatic transmission.

F Complete each sentence with <u>something</u> or <u>anything</u>.

1. We have _____ new at our salon.
2. He didn't take _____ for his headache.
3. Do you need _____ from the drugstore?
4. I didn't see _____ I like in the catalog.
5. I always buy _____ from that store.
6. I just can't relax. There is always _____ to do.
7. They gave me _____ to drink at the salon.
8. I don't know _____ about cosmetic surgery.

G Read the paragraph. Find and correct five mistakes.

> I went to the supermarket today because I needed to get nothing to cook for my dinner party tonight. I wanted to buy some juice, too. But when I got there, there wasn't nothing on the shelf! I went to the store manager and asked him why the shelves were empty. He apologized and said there was anything wrong with the delivery truck. "It didn't come today," he told me. He said I'd have to wait until the next day. Now I don't have something to serve for the big party tonight. I've never seen nothing like this!

WRITING BOOSTER

A Think about a time when you had bad service at a place of business such as a salon, a car rental agency, a hotel, a movie theater, or a restaurant. Write an e-mail message to the manager complaining about the service. Describe the problem you had. Suggest a way for the business to improve.

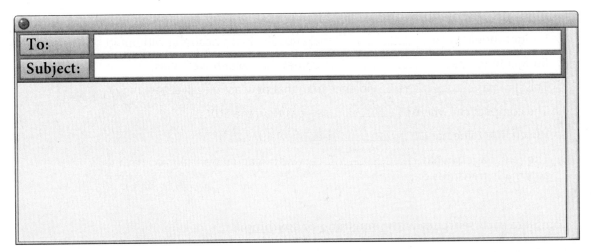

B Prepare to turn your e-mail message into a formal business letter. Write the following information.

1. your address: _____

2. recipient's name and / or position and address:

   _____

3. today's date: _____

4. a salutation: _____

5. a complimentary close: _____

6. your signature and printed name: _____

C Now type (or write) your formal business letter. Use the e-mail message you wrote in Exercise A as the body of your letter. Include all the information from Exercise B.

ABOUT THE AUTHORS

Joan Saslow

Joan Saslow has taught in a variety of programs in South America and the United States. She is author or coauthor of a number of widely used courses, some of which are *Ready to Go, Workplace Plus, Literacy Plus,* and *Summit.* She is also author of *English in Context,* a series for reading science and technology. Ms. Saslow was the series director of *True Colors* and *True Voices.* She has participated in the English Language Specialist Program in the U.S. Department of State's Bureau of Educational and Cultural Affairs.

Allen Ascher

Allen Ascher has been a teacher and teacher trainer in China and the United States, as well as academic director of the intensive English program at Hunter College. Mr. Ascher has also been an ELT publisher and was responsible for publication and expansion of numerous well-known courses including *True Colors, NorthStar,* the *Longman TOEFL Preparation Series,* and the *Longman Academic Writing Series.* He is coauthor of *Summit,* and he wrote the "Teaching Speaking" module of *Teacher Development Interactive,* an online multimedia teacher-training program.

Ms. Saslow and Mr. Ascher are frequent presenters at professional conferences and have been coauthoring courses for teens, adults, and young adults since 2002.

AUTHORS' ACKNOWLEDGMENTS

The authors are indebted to these reviewers, who provided extensive and detailed feedback and suggestions for *Top Notch,* as well as the hundreds of teachers who completed surveys and participated in focus groups.

Manuel Wilson Alvarado Miles, Quito, Ecuador • **Shirley Ando,** Otemae University, Hyogo, Japan • **Vanessa de Andrade,** CCBEU Inter Americano, Curitiba, Brazil • **Miguel Arrazola,** CBA, Santa Cruz, Bolivia • **Mark Barta,** Proficiency School of English, São Paulo, Brazil • **Edwin Bello,** PROULEX, Guadalajara, Mexico • **Mary Blum,** CBA, Cochabamba, Bolivia • **María Elizabeth Boccia,** Proficiency School of English, São Paulo, Brazil • **Pamela Cristina Borja Baltán,** Quito, Ecuador • **Eliana Anabel L. Buccia,** AMICANA, Mendoza, Argentina • **José Humberto Calderón Díaz,** CALUSAC, Guatemala City, Guatemala • **María Teresa Calienes Csirke,** Idiomas Católica, Lima, Peru • **Esther María Carbo Morales,** Quito, Ecuador • **Jorge Washington Cárdenas Castillo,** Quito, Ecuador • **Eréndira Yadira Carrera García,** UVM Chapultepec, Mexico City, Mexico • **Viviane de Cássia Santos Carlini,** Spectrum Line, Pouso Alegre, Brazil • **Centro Colombo Americano,** Bogota, Colombia • **Guven Ciftci,** Fatih University, Istanbul, Turkey • **Diego Cisneros,** CBA, Tarija, Bolivia • **Paul Crook,** Meisei University, Tokyo, Japan • **Alejandra Díaz Loo,** El Cultural, Arequipa, Peru • **Jesús G. Díaz Osío,** Florida National College, Miami, USA • **María Eid Ceneviva,** CBA, Bolivia • **Amalia Elvira Rodríguez Espinoza De Los Monteros,** Guayaquil, Ecuador • **María Argelia Estrada Vásquez,** CALUSAC, Guatemala City, Guatemala • **John Fieldeldy,** College of Engineering, Nihon University, Aizuwakamatsu-shi, Japan • **Marleni Humbelina Flores Urízar,** CALUSAC, Guatemala City, Guatemala • **Gonzalo Fortune,** CBA, Sucre, Bolivia • **Andrea Fredricks,** Embassy CES, San Francisco, USA • **Irma Gallegos Peláez,** UVM Tlalpan, Mexico City, Mexico • **Alberto Gamarra,** CBA, Santa Cruz, Bolivia • **María Amparo García Peña,** ICPNA Cusco, Peru • **Amanda Gillis-Furutaka,** Kyoto Sangyo University, Kyoto, Japan • **Martha Angelina González**

Párraga, Guayaquil, Ecuador • **Octavio Garduño Ruiz,** Business Training Consultant, Mexico City, Mexico • **Ralph Grayson,** Idiomas Católica, Lima, Peru • **Murat Gultekin,** Fatih University, Istanbul, Turkey • **Oswaldo Gutiérrez,** PROULEX, Guadalajara, Mexico • **Ayaka Hashinishi,** Otemae University, Hyogo, Japan • **Alma Lorena Hernández de Armas,** CALUSAC, Guatemala City, Guatemala • **Kent Hill,** Seigakuin University, Saitama-ken, Japan • **Kayoko Hirao,** Nichii Gakkan Company, COCO Juku, Japan • **Jesse Huang,** National Central University, Taoyuan, Taiwan • **Eric Charles Jones,** Seoul University of Technology, Seoul, South Korea • **Jun-Chen Kuo,** Tajen University, Pingtung , Taiwan • **Susan Krieger,** Embassy CES, San Francisco, USA • **Ana María de la Torre Ugarte,** ICPNA Chiclayo, Peru • **Erin Lemaistre,** Chung-Ang University, Seoul, South Korea • **Eleanor S. Leu,** Soochow University, Taipei, Taiwan • **Yihui Li (Stella Li),** Fooyin University, Kaohsiung, Taiwan • **Chin-Fan Lin,** Shih Hsin University, Taipei, Taiwan • **Linda Lin,** Tatung Institute of Technology, Taiwan • **Kristen Lindblom,** Embassy CES, San Francisco, USA • **Patricio David López Logacho,** Quito, Ecuador • **Diego López Tasara,** Idiomas Católica, Lima, Peru • **Neil Macleod,** Kansai Gaidai University, Osaka, Japan • **Adriana Marcés,** Idiomas Católica, Lima, Peru • **Robyn McMurray,** Pusan National University, Busan, South Korea • **Paula Medina,** London Language Institute, London, Canada • **Juan Carlos Muñoz,** American School Way, Bogota, Colombia • **Noriko Mori,** Otemae University, Hyogo, Japan • **Adrián Esteban Narváez Pacheco,** Cuenca, Ecuador • **Tim Newfields,** Tokyo University Faculty of Economics, Tokyo, Japan • **Ana Cristina Ochoa,** CCBEU Inter Americano, Curitiba, Brazil • **Tania Elizabeth Ortega Santacruz,** Cuenca, Ecuador • **Martha Patricia Páez,** Quito, Ecuador • **María de Lourdes Pérez Valdespino,** Universidad del Valle

de México, Mexico • **Wahrena Elizabeth Pfeister,** University of Suwon, Gyeonggi-Do, South Korea • **Wayne Allen Pfeister,** University of Suwon, Gyeonggi-Do, South Korea • **Andrea Rebonato,** CCBEU Inter Americano, Curitiba, Brazil • **Thomas Robb,** Kyoto Sangyo University, Kyoto, Japan • **Mehran Sabet,** Seigakuin University, Saitama-ken, Japan • **Majid Safadaran Mosazadeh,** ICPNA Chiclayo, Peru • **Timothy Samuelson,** BridgeEnglish, Denver, USA • **Héctor Sánchez,** PROULEX, Guadalajara, Mexico • **Mónica Alexandra Sánchez Escalante,** Quito, Ecuador • **Jorge Mauricio Sánchez Montalván,** Quito, Universidad Politécnica Salesiana (UPS), Ecuador • **Letícia Santos,** ICBEU Ibiá, Brazil • **Elena Sapp,** INTO Oregon State University, Corvallis, USA • **Robert Sheridan,** Otemae University, Hyogo, Japan • **John Eric Sherman,** Hong Ik University, Seoul, South Korea • **Brooks Slaybaugh,** Asia University, Tokyo, Japan • **João Vitor Soares,** NACC, São Paulo, Brazil • **Silvia Solares,** CBA, Sucre, Bolivia • **Chayawan Sonchaeng,** Delaware County Community College, Media, PA • **María Julia Suárez,** CBA, Cochabamba, Bolivia • **Elena Sudakova,** English Language Center, Kiev, Ukraine • **Richard Swingle,** Kansai Gaidai College, Osaka, Japan • **Blanca Luz Terrazas Zamora,** ICPNA Cusco, Peru • **Sandrine Ting,** St. John's University, New Taipei City, Taiwan • **Christian Juan Torres Medina,** Guayaquil, Ecuador • **Raquel Torrico,** CBA, Sucre, Bolivia • **Jessica Ueno,** Otemae University, Hyogo, Japan • **Ximena Vacaflor C.,** CBA, Tarija, Bolivia • **René Valdivia Pereira,** CBA, Santa Cruz, Bolivia • **Solange Lopes Vinagre Costa,** SENAC, São Paulo, Brazil • **Magno Alejandro Vivar Hurtado,** Cuenca, Ecuador • **Dr. Wen-hsien Yang,** National Kaohsiung Hospitality College, Kaohsiung, Taiwan • **Juan Zárate,** El Cultural, Arequipa, Peru